H. De Romestin

The Teaching of the Twelve Apostles

Second Edition

H. De Romestin

The Teaching of the Twelve Apostles
Second Edition

ISBN/EAN: 9783744675864

Printed in Europe, USA, Canada, Australia, Japan

Cover: Foto ©Lupo / pixelio.de

More available books at **www.hansebooks.com**

The Teaching of the Twelve Apostles.

ΔΙΔΑΧΗ ΤΩΝ ΔΩΔΕΚΑ ΑΠΟΣΤΟΛΩΝ.

WITH

INTRODUCTION, TRANSLATION, NOTES, AND ILLUSTRATIVE PASSAGES.

EDITED BY

H. DE ROMESTIN, M.A.

VICAR OF STONY STRATFORD.

Second Edition.

Parker and Co.

OXFORD, AND 6 SOUTHAMPTON-STREET,
STRAND, LONDON.

1885.

TO

THE REV. GEORGE NOEL FREELING, M.A.

FELLOW OF MERTON COLLEGE,

VICAR OF HOLYWELL, OXFORD, AND RURAL DEAN.

IN GRATITUDE FOR

A FRIENDSHIP OF MORE THAN FORTY YEARS.

October, 1884.

PREFACE TO SECOND EDITION.

In preparing this Second Edition of the Διδαχή for the press the Editor has corrected a few misprints, but has made no further alterations. He may, however, say that his conviction as to a *very* early date for the treatise (perhaps A.D. 60—70) is much strengthened. But this may possibly not apply to the whole writing.

The following additional matter has come to his knowledge :—

A Translation, with notes, &c., by Professor G. Bonet-Maury. Paris, 1884.

An Edition, with notes, &c., by Canon Spence. London, 1885.

Another, with notes, &c., by M. Paul Sabatier. Paris, 1885.

And notices in reviews and periodicals, of which the chief are,—

Bapheides in Ἐκκλησιαστικὴ ἀλήθεια. 1884.

Four writers in the *Journal of Christian Philosophy* (American).

Ménégoz in *Le Temoignage*. 1884-5.

Krawutzky, *Tübinger Quartal Schrift*. 1884, iv.

Holtzmann, *Jahrbücher f. prot. Theologie*.

And some others of less importance.

For the subjoined notice of Abp. Bryennius, which may be interesting to many, the Editor is indebted to the edition of M. Sabatier mentioned above, to whom

b

the facts were obligingly communicated by the Archbishop's secretary.

"Philotheus Bryennius was born in 1833 at Constantinople, at the theological college of which city he was educated. After distinguished success in his course he proceeded to study for four years and a half at the Universities of Leipzig, Berlin, and Munich.

"On his return to Constantinople he was appointed tutor of his theological college, of which he soon after became the head, and at the same time Dean of the School of the Phanar, where is the Library of the Holy Sepulchre.

"After this date (1868) he became known for his theological attainments, spirit of wide enquiry, and large sympathies. Together with the Metropolitan of Cæsarea he represented the Church of Constantinople at the Old Catholic Congress at Bonn in 1872, during the progress of which he was appointed Metropolitan of Serræ, and two years later was promoted to Nicomedia, the see over which he now presides."

Easter, 1885.

PREFACE TO FIRST EDITION.

THE preparation of the following pages has been a labour of love, owing to the deeply interesting nature of the short treatise here presented to the public. But whilst claiming to have spared no pains in the task, the Editor does not pretend to do more than present to the English reader what may, he trusts, prove to be a handbook to what has been already done, leaving deeper investigations to the labours of learned critics and Church historians.

The text adopted in the following pages, represents the MS. readings of the original, as gathered from the first edition of Bryennius, and some further communications of his to different critics.

In ch. iii. ver. 9, however, it has not been thought necessary to retain the MS. readings, τῇι and ἀναστραφήσηι; though the former of these occurs singularly enough in the corresponding passage of Barnabas, ch. xix. in the same MS. And in some few places also the punctuation has been tacitly corrected or modified.

Besides this edition, those of Harnack and Hilgenfeld have been carefully gone through, as well as the shorter works of Wünsche, and of Professors Hitchcock and Brown of New York, besides many translations and reviews, English and foreign.

Bryennius informs us that the treatise is written consecutively with no breaks, or capital letters after the first word, and there are also the usual contractions.

The division into chapters is taken from Bryennius, that into verses or paragraphs from Harnack. Unfortunately Hilgenfeld, in his edition of the Διδαχή, has adopted another system as regards the verses.

In the Notes at the foot of the Text, B. stands for Bryennius; Hr. for Harnack (*Texte und Untersuchungen*, vol. ii. pts. 1 and 2); Hl. for Hilgenfeld (*Nov. Can. extra Textum receptum*).

The Translation, as a rule, follows the original text, occasionally, however, it follows the emendations.

The following is a list of editions which have been, more or less, made use of by the Editor, and to this is appended a list of reviews, criticisms, and the like, nearly all of which have been consulted.

The *Editio princeps* of Bryennius, with notes and valuable prolegomena. Constantinople, 1883.

An Edition with translation, notes, and prolegomena by Harnack. *Texte und Untersuchungen*, Vol. II. Pts. 1 and 2. Leipzig, 1884.

Another, with notes, &c., by Hilgenfeld. *Nov. Test. ext. Can. recept.*, Ed. II. Fasc. 4. Leipzig, 1884.

Another, with notes, &c., by Wünsche. Leipzig, 1884.

Another, with notes, &c., by Professors Hitchcock and Brown. New York, 1884.

Among reviews, criticisms, and translations, are the following noted by the Editor.

J. W. in *Guardian*, March 19.

E. L. H., *Guardian*, June 25.

Farrar, *Contemporary Review*, also *Expositor*, May.

Robertson, *Durham University Journal*, February.

Swainson, *Churchman*, February.

Plummer, *Churchman*, July.

Howson, *Churchman*, August.

Harnack, in Schürer's *Theolog. Lit. Zeitung, III.*

Hilgenfeld, *Zeitschrift f. wissentsch. Theologie*, p. 371.

Journal of Christian Philosophy (American).

Stokes, *Contemporary Review*, April.

Funk, *Zeitschr. f. Kath. Theologie II.*, also *Tübinger Quartal Schrift. III.*

Prins, Διδαχὴ τῶν δώδεκα ἀποστόλων in usum studiosæ juventutis repet. Lugd. Bat.

Warming, *De tolv apostles laerdom*, Kopenhagen.

Boase, *Academy*, Ap. 19.

Zahn. Die Lehre, &c., in *Forschungen zur Geschichte des N. T. Kanons*, Pt. III.

Bryennius [A letter] *Andover Review*, June (American).

Muralt E. de, *Revue de Theologie et de Philosophie*, May.

Duchesne, *Bulletin critique*, March.

Articles in *New Englander* (American), July.

Lobb's *Theological Quarterly*, Pt. III.

All these, except the Constantinople Edition of the Διδαχή, have appeared during the present year. There have been also a number of letters in the *Guardian* and in other newspapers.

The thanks of the Editor for kind answers to en-
quiries are due to the Dean of Canterbury, and to
Mr. E. Thompson, of the MS. department, British
Museum.

In order, however, to make the work more complete,
and to exhibit more clearly the relationship of the
Διδαχή to other documents, it has been thought well to
append certain extracts by way of Illustrations.

First of all, those passages of Holy Scripture, which
the Διδαχή seems either to follow, or to which it may
be supposed incidentally to allude.

Next, some passages from the Epistle of Barnabas,
and a short piece of Hermas, with which, as will be
seen by the Introduction, the comparison has raised an
interesting question as to priority of date.

And there is also added an existing fragment (unfortunately very brief) of an early Latin translation of
the Διδαχή.

But, further, the material of the writing before us
seems to have been used in other documents of later,
but still very early, date, extracts from which are,
therefore, appended.

1. The "Ecclesiastical Canons of the Holy Apostles," called also, Ἐπιτομὴ ὅρων τῶν ἁγίων ἀποστόλων.

2. An English translation of a Coptic version of the
same Ecclesiastical Canons.

3. Part of the Seventh Book of the Apostolical Constitutions.

The contents of the work will, therefore, stand as
follows:—

CONTENTS.

INTRODUCTION.

SOME years since Philotheus Bryennius, then Metropolitan of Serræ, in Macedonia, since translated to Nicomedia, discovered in the Library of the Most Holy Sepulchre, belonging to the Patriarchate of Jerusalem at Constantinople, a MS. written at Jerusalem, A.D. 1056, containing: 1. St. Chrysostom's Synopsis of the Old Testament; 2. The Epistle of Barnabas; 3. The First Epistle of St. Clement of Rome to the Corinthians; 4. The Second Epistle (spurious); 5. The Teaching of the Apostles; 6. The Epistle of Mary of Cassobolæ to St. Ignatius (spurious); 7. Twelve Epistles of St. Ignatius (partly spurious). The volume bears the library mark, No. 456, is of parchment, small 8vo., eight inches by seven nearly, and was completed, according to an inscription at the end, on June 11, A.D. 1056, by a notary named Leo.

A copy of No. 2 was sent to Hilgenfeld, and used for his new edition of the Epistle of Barnabas, 1877, and utilized by Gebhardt and Harnack, *Patres App.*, 1878. Funk received a copy of the Ignatian Epistles, No. 7, for his edition of the Apostolical Fathers, 1881. Bryennius himself edited St. Clement, Nos. 3 and 4, and his edition has been used by Bishop Lightfoot.

No. 5 in the above list is a short treatise bearing the title, "Teaching of the Twelve Apostles," which Bryennius edited and published, with copious learned notes and prolegomena, at Constantinople, towards the end of 1883.

B

This is not the least important of the contents of
the MS., throwing as it does a light upon the life and
state of feeling of the Christian Church in the latter
half of the first, or, at latest, the beginning of the second, century of the Christian era.

Who the compiler may have been is wholly unknown, but a large part of the subject-matter is found,
often word for word, in parts of the Epistle of Barnabas, the Shepherd of Hermas, in the seventh book
and other parts of the so-called Apostolical Constitutions, a work of the third and following centuries;
and in other treatises of a similar character. Parts of
some of these, with what remains of an early Latin
version, are printed in this volume.

The work contains moral precepts, some rules as to
Prayer, Fasting, Baptism and the Eucharist, and the
Teachers of the Church, and ends with a solemn refer-
ence to the Coming of the Lord and the Resurrection.

We may take some of these points rather more in
detail.

There is not much to guide us in determining who,
or of what nation the writer was. A few Hebraisms
may point to a Jewish Christian; but if this be the
case there are, on the one hand, no signs of Ebionite
hostility to St. Paul, nor, on the other, any signs of
the influence of some special points of his teaching,
nor clear references to his writings. Perhaps the
writer may have lived in Asia Minor, the Eucharistic
prayers shewing traces of St. John's language, though
such occur nowhere else; and the special notices of
magic in some detail in ch. iii. 4, and v. 1, shew
possibly a tendency to the "curious arts" which the

converts forsook at Ephesus when they burned their books (Acts xix. 19). Harnack, *Texte und Untersuch-ungen,* vol. ii. p. 159 ; Funk, in the *Tübinger Quartal Schrift,* 1884, p. 382, and others, refer it, and with more probability, to Egypt, chiefly on the ground of its close connection with the Epistle of Barnabas. Egypt, moreover, would seem more likely from the later settlement of the Church in that country, and the distance from St. Paul's teaching, whilst magic abounded no less. The first mention, too, after this treatise, of the Wednesday and Friday fast is in St. Clement of Alexandria, Strom. vii. 75.

As to the date, the work is cited as Scripture by Clement of Alexandria ᵃ, who died *c.* A.D. 217; and any further deduction must depend on the answer given to the question whether Barnabas and Hermas were sources or copies of the "Teaching." Most authori-ties, e.g. Bryennius, Harnack, and Hilgenfeld, consider the "Teaching" to be the later ᵇ; but Funk (*Tübinger Quartal Schrift,* 1884, pt. iii.), pointing out that there is no absolute proof, contests this view, first as to Her-mas, that the verbal coincidences may just as well lead to the conclusion that Hermas copied, which would also be the more likely, inasmuch as the "Teaching" being a work written for instruction, might very well be thus utilized.

As to the Epistle of Barnabas, at first sight the prob-ability seems to be that the "Teaching" is a more

---

ᵃ See note on Διδαχή, iii. 5.

ᵇ Zahn, *Forschungen,* &c., considers that the Διδαχή prob-ably copied Hermas, but not Barnabas.

orderly arrangement of passages taken from the Epistle. But each has some sentences omitted in the other, and the "Teaching" has specially two portions of some length altogether wanting in Barnabas, viz., ch. i. 2, to the end, i.e. the greater part of the chapter (also wanting in the Latin version), and the whole section, contained in ch. iii. 1—6.

Then in the "Teaching" the two commandments, love of God and of our neighbour, stand together at the commencement: in Barnabas they are separated, and the remaining commandments, more or less exactly, grouped under them. But perhaps the point which lends most probability to the view that our work may be the original, is the singular dislocation of the sentence, ch. iv. 13, which appears in two different places in ch. xix. of Barnabas: first, *v.* 2, "Thou shalt not forsake the commandments of the Lord;" and then, after a considerable interval, *v.* 30, "Thou shalt keep what thou hast received, neither adding nor taking away."

But, whichever of the two writings be the earlier, there is nothing in the way of external evidence to bring the date of the work before us, with any certainty, so low as the earliest part of the second century; What, then, can we infer from internal evidence?

1. There is no sign of any Canon of the New Testament, only the "Gospel" or the "Commandment of the Lord" is referred to, most often according to St. Matthew, sometimes St. Luke, seldom quite word for word; sometimes a text agreeing with neither, but in a few instances with Tatian's Diatessaron. There are one or two points which would go to support a

theory that the writer was contemporary with St. Paul, and heard of some of his teaching; but it does not at all appear that even the earliest Epistles were known to him as writings.

2. The office-bearers of the Church still have the titles used in the New Testament (except that Evangelist seems merged in Apostle, and Presbyter is omitted), even that of Apostle being not yet confined to the Twelve; while the chief work seems to be preaching and instruction, for the purpose of conversion, no doubt; and prophets hold an important position.

3. The ἀγάπη seems to be not yet disjoined from the Eucharist, if indeed every meal has not somewhat of an Eucharistic character.

4. There is no trace, any more than in the New Testament, of a long preparation for Baptism, or of a class of Catechumens; and, as in the only case mentioned in the New Testament of a Christian falling into deadly sin, and repenting, so in this "Teaching of the Lord through the Apostles," the impenitent sinner, indeed, is to abstain from communion, but so soon as he repents and confesses he is apparently, with no long period of probation, admitted again to his full privileges.

Again, one very singular feature to be considered is that the week in the Διδαχή is fully arranged, with the exception of Saturday, as in later times: Sunday with its services, Wednesday and Friday with their fasts; but there is no sign of any yearly festival or fast as being yet instituted. Now the Lord's day is already observed in the times of the New Testament (Acts

xx. 7; 1 Cor. xvi. 2); whilst in the middle of the
second century there is a dispute as to the right time
for celebrating Easter (which must therefore already
have been some time observed). It would seem that
the Διδαχή must synchronize with the former state of
affairs rather than with the latter.

So we conclude, that whilst the origin of the work
before us is uncertain as to its locality, there is absolutely nothing to prevent our assigning as its date
possibly (if not probably) the last quarter of the first,
certainly nothing later than the earlier quarter of the
second, century. It may well be the oldest Christian
writing after the books of the New Testament[c], perhaps even earlier than most of them.

The subject-matter is the simplest of practical teaching, such as may well have been current in similar
forms, and being taught orally and then committed to
memory by those who had to teach others, was written
down by some teacher in the form which we have in
the Διδαχή.

Oral teaching must have been the rule, to which
St. Luke bears something like witness, writing, ch. i. 3,
to Theophilus, ἵνα ἐπιγνῷς περὶ ὧν κατηχήθης λόγων τὴν
ἀσφάλειαν. And St. Augustine appears to refer to the
custom of learning by heart for the purpose of instruct-
ing others, when, De Catechizandis rudibus, ch. v., he
warns the Catechist against being too prolix, and says

---

[c] Archdeacon Farrar is also of opinion that the Διδαχή is
older than the Epistle of Barnabas or Hermas. Prebendary
Sadler ("Guardian," June 4, 1884,) and H. L. W. ("Guardian,"
June 26), both support a very early date; and the latter also
supposes the Διδαχή to be the original of Barnabas' Epistle.

we must not "si ad verbum edidicimus, memoriter reddere" whole books of the Bible.

Another point of interest is to notice how later ecclesiastical documents, such as the Ecclesiastical Canons and Apostolical Constitutions, introduce changes in the subject-matter of the Διδαχή to suit the circumstances of the Church and times. For instance, διδάσκαλοι, or, as in x. 7, προφῆται become πρεσβύτεροι in Ap. Const. vii. 26; ἐμπλησθῆναι, ch. x. 1, is changed into μετάληψιν in Ap. Const. vii. 26.

Or again, in treating of Baptism, the addition of the "ἐπίσκοπε ἢ πρεσβύτερε," as ministers; and as to the ceremonies, "χρίσεις ἐλαίῳ ἁγίῳ," in Ap. Const. vii. 22.

Very noticeable, too, is the subsequent omission of the direction for public Confession before Communion, which has no place in later Eastern Liturgies. It is as though the work was, from time to time, revised to bring it up to date, and then the old editions which would have testified to later changes and corruptions were allowed to drop into oblivion.

A SUMMARY OF THE Διδαχή.

Part I. Brief rules of Christian morality, and the
duties of individuals.

A. The way of life {
1. Love of God (*not fully worked out*).
2. Love of our neighbour.
}

  1. The love of God in two directions.

    (*a.*) Love of God as Creator, and then (apparently founded on St. Matt. v. 44)

    (*b.*) Love of enemies for God's sake, "that ye may be the children of your Father which is in heaven, for He maketh His sun to rise on the evil and on the good, and sendeth rain on the just and the unjust." ch. i.

  2. The love of our neighbour based upon the commandments of the second Table in various practical duties, ending with the injunction to confess transgressions, and not come to prayer with an evil conscience. ch. ii.—iv.

B. The way of death. A catalogue of sins, with the warning not to be led astray from the right way of teaching. ch. v., vi. 1.

  A parenthetical injunction, "if thou art not able to bear the whole yoke of the Lord, do what thou canst," and a similar one concerning fasting. ch. vi. 2, 3.

PART II. Duties as Members of the Church.

C. Church discipline {
1. Matters.
2. Persons.

1. Matters connected with Christian life and teaching.

(a) Baptism, ch. vii.; (b) Fasting; and (c) Prayer, ch. viii. (d) The Eucharist, ch. ix., x.

2. The persons connected with Christian life and teaching.

Teachers, Apostles, Prophets, Ordinary Christians. ch. xi., xii.

3. Special duties of congregations { Persons,
regarding { Worship.

a. Duties as to the support of the prophets. ch. xiii.

b. Duties as to Sunday observances. ch. xiv.; and (apparently as resulting from the latter)
The appointment of bishops and deacons. ch. xv.

CONCLUSION.

An earnest exhortation and warning.
1. As to the increase of evil in the latter days.
2. The coming of the Lord. ch. xvi.

PASSAGES OF HOLY SCRIPTURE QUOTED IN, OR
SIMILAR TO, PASSAGES CONTAINED IN THE
Διδαχὴ τῶν δώδεκα ἀποστόλων.

ALL the striking passages are here given, but the
writer of the Διδαχή seems in several other places to
have had the Old Testament in view, for instance in
ch. xiii., where he is giving rules as to first-fruits.
Enough are however given to shew that he seldom
quotes a passage as it stands in the Septuagint.

For the New Testament the same remark applies,
and the reader may form his own conclusions as to
whether the writer had St. Matthew's Gospel in view,
or was quoting from some 'εὐαγγέλιον' which was
orally current.

The Scriptural illustrations are arranged in parallel
columns with the passages of the Διδαχή; and references are given to chapter and verse both of the Διδαχή
and of Scripture.

Διδαχή.	Scripture.
i. 2. πάντα δὲ ὅσα ἐὰν θελήσῃς μὴ γένεσθαί σοι, καὶ σὺ ἄλλῳ μὴ ποίει.	Tobit iv. 15. καὶ ὅ μισεῖς, μηδενὶ ποιήσῃς.
iii. 8. γίνου . . . ἡσύχιος καὶ ἀγαθὸς καὶ τρέμων τοὺς λόγους διὰ παντός, οὓς ἤκουσας.	Isaiah lxvi. 2. [ἐπιβλέψω] ἐπὶ τὸν ταπεινὸν καὶ ἡσύχιον, καὶ τρέμοντα τοὺς λόγους μου.

Διδαχή.

iii. 10. τὰ συμβαίνοντά σοι ἐνεργήματα ὡς ἀγαθὰ προσδέξῃ.

iv. 5. μὴ γίνου πρὸς μὲν τὸ λαβεῖν ἐκτείνων τὰς χεῖρας, πρὸς δὲ τὸ δοῦναι συσπῶν.

iv. 6. ἐὰν ἔχῃς ... δώσεις λύτρωσιν ἁμαρτιῶν σου.

iv. 6, 7, 8. ... οὐ διστάσεις δοῦναι, οὐδὲ διδοὺς γογγύσεις ... οὐκ ἀποστραφήσῃ τὸν ἐνδεόμενον·

iv. 13. φυλάξεις ἃ παρέλαβες, μήτε προστιθεὶς μήτε ἀφαιρῶν.

xiv. 3. ἐν παντὶ τόπῳ καὶ χρόνῳ προσφέρειν μοι θυσίαν καθαράν· ὅτι βασιλεὺς μέγας εἰμί, λέγει Κύριος, καὶ τὸ ὄνομά μου θαυμαστὸν ἐν τοῖς ἔθνεσι.

xvi. 7. ἥξει ὁ Κύριος καὶ πάντες οἱ ἅγιοι μετ' αὐτοῦ.

Scripture.

Ecclus. ii. 4. πᾶν ὃ ἐὰν ἐπαχθῇ σοι, δέξαι.

Ecclus. iv. 31. μὴ ἔστω ἡ χείρ σου ἐκτεταμένη εἰς τὸ λαβεῖν, καὶ ἐν τῷ ἀποδιδόναι συνεσταλμένη.

Daniel iv. 27. τὰς ἀδικίας [ἁμαρτίας, Theodot.] σου ἐν ἐλεημοσύναις λύτρωσαι.

Tobit iv. 7. ἐκ τῶν ὑπαρχόντων σου ποίει ἐλεημοσύνην, καὶ μὴ φθονεσάτω σου ὁ ὀφθαλμὸς ἐν τῷ ποιεῖν σε ἐλεημοσύνην· μὴ ἀποστρέψῃς τὸ πρόσωπόν σου ἀπὸ παντὸς πτωχοῦ.

Ecclus. iv. 5. ἀπὸ δεομένου μὴ ἀποστρέψῃς ὀφθαλμόν.

Deut. xii. 32. πᾶν ῥῆμα ... φυλάξῃ ποιεῖν, οὐ προσθήσεις ἐπ' αὐτό, οὐδὲ ἀφελεῖς ἀπ' αὐτοῦ.

Mal. i. 11, 14. ἐν παντὶ τόπῳ θυμίαμα προσάγεται τῷ ὀνόματί μου, καὶ θυσία καθαρά· διότι μέγα τὸ ὄνομά μου ἐν τοῖς ἔθνεσι λέγει Κύριος παντοκράτωρ.

Zech. xiv. 8. ἥξει Κύριος ὁ Θεός μου, καὶ πάντες οἱ ἅγιοι μετ' αὐτοῦ.

Διδαχή.	Scripture.
i. 2. πρῶτον, ἀγαπήσεις τὸν Θεὸν τὸν ποιήσαντά σε· δεύτερον, τὸν πλησίον σου ὡς σεαυτόν. '	Matt. xxii. 37. ἀγαπήσεις Κύριον τὸν Θεόν σου ... αὕτη ἐστὶν ἡ μεγάλη καὶ πρώτη ἐντολή. δευτέρα ... ἀγαπήσεις τὸν πλησίον σοῦ ὡς σεαυτόν.
i. 2. πάντα δὲ ὅσα ἐὰν θελήσῃς μὴ γίνεσθαί σοι, καὶ σὺ ἄλλῳ μὴ ποίει.	Matt. vii. 12. πάντα οὖν ὅσα ἐὰν θέλητε ἵνα ποιῶσιν ὑμῖν οἱ ἄνθρωποι, οὕτως καὶ ὑμεῖς ποιεῖτε αὐτοῖς. Luke vi. 31. καὶ καθὼς θέλετε ἵνα ποιῶσιν ἡμῖν οἱ ἄνθρωποι, ποιεῖτε αὐτοῖς ὁμοίως.
i. 3. Εὐλογεῖτε τοὺς καταρωμένους ὑμῖν καὶ προσεύχεσθε ὑπὲρ τῶν ἐχθρῶν ὑμῶν, νησεύετε δὲ ὑπὲρ τῶν διωκόντων ὑμᾶς· ποία γὰρ χάρις, ἐὰν ἀγαπᾶτε τοὺς ἀγαπῶντας ὑμᾶς; οὐχὶ καὶ τὰ ἔθνη τὸ αὐτὸ ποιοῦσιν; ὑμεῖς δὲ ἀγαπᾶτε τοὺς μισοῦντας ὑμᾶς καὶ οὐχ ἕξετε ἐχθρόν.	Matt. v. 44, 46. προσεύχεσθε ὑπὲρ τῶν διωκόντων ὑμᾶς ... ἐὰν γὰρ ἀγαπήσητε τοὺς ἀγαπῶντας ὑμᾶς, τίνα μισθὸν ἔχετε; ... οὐχὶ καὶ οἱ ἐθνικοὶ τὸ αὐτὸ ποιοῦσιν; Luke vi. 27, 28, 32, 35. Εὐλογεῖτε τοὺς καταρωμένους ὑμᾶς, προσεύχεσθε περὶ τῶν ἐπηρεαζόντων ὑμᾶς ... καὶ εἰ ἀγαπᾶτε τοὺς ἀγαπῶντας ὑμᾶς, ποία ὑμῖν χάρις ἐστίν; καὶ γὰρ οἱ ἁμαρτωλοὶ τοὺς ἀγαπῶντας αὐτοὺς ἀγαπῶσιν ... πλὴν ἀγαπᾶτε τοὺς ἐχθροὺς ὑμῶν.

Διδαχή.

i. 4. ἀπέχου τῶν σαρκικῶν καὶ σωματικῶν ἐπιθυμιῶν.

i. 4. Ἐάν τις σοι δῷ ῥάπισμα εἰς τὴν δεξιὰν σιαγόνα, στρέψον αὐτῷ καὶ τὴν ἄλλην, καὶ ἔσῃ τέλειος· ἐάν ἀγγαρεύσῃ σέ τις μίλιον ἕν, ὕπαγε μετ' αὐτοῦ δύο· ἐὰν ἄρῃ τις τὸ ἱμάτιόν σου, δὸς αὐτῷ καὶ τὸν χιτῶνα· ἐὰν λάβῃ τις ἀπὸ σοῦ τὸ σόν, μὴ ἀπαίτει· οὐδὲ γὰρ δύνασαι.

Scripture.

1 Pet. ii. 11. ἀπέχεσθαι τῶν σαρκικῶν ἐπιθυμιῶν.

Matt. v. 39—41. ὅστις σε ῥαπίζει εἰς τὴν δεξιὰν σιαγόνα, στρέψον αὐτῷ καὶ τὴν ἄλλην· καὶ τῷ θέλοντί σοι κριθῆναι καὶ τὸν χιτῶνά σου λαβεῖν, ἄφες αὐτῷ καὶ τὸ ἱμάτιον· καὶ ὅστις σε ἀγγαρεύσει μίλιον ἕν, ὕπαγε μετ' αὐτοῦ δύο.

Luke vi. 29, 30. τῷ τύπτοντί σε ἐπὶ τὴν σιαγόνα πάρεχε καὶ τὴν ἄλλην, καὶ ἀπὸ τοῦ αἴροντός σου τὸ ἱμάτιον καὶ τὸν χιτῶνα μὴ κωλύσῃς . . . ἀπὸ τοῦ αἴροντος τὰ σὰ μὴ ἀπαίτει.

i. 5. Παντὶ τῷ αἰτοῦντί σε δίδου καὶ μὴ ἀπαίτει.

Matt. v. 42. τῷ αἰτοῦντί σε δίδου.

Luke vi. 30. παντὶ αἰτοῦντί σε δίδου καὶ . . . μὴ ἀπαίτει.

i. 5. ἐν συνοχῇ δὲ γενόμενος ἐξετασθήσεται περὶ ὧν ἔπραξε, καὶ οὐκ ἐξελεύσεται ἐκεῖθεν μέχρις οὗ ἀποδῷ τὸν ἔσχατον κοδράντην.

Matt. v. 26. ἀμὴν λέγω σοι, οὐ μὴ ἐξέλθῃς ἐκεῖθεν ἕως ἂν ἀποδῷς τὸν ἔσχατον κοδράντην.

iii. 7. Ἴσθι πραΰς, ἐπεὶ οἱ πραεῖς κληρονομήσουσι τὴν γῆν.

Matt. v. 5. μακάριοι οἱ πραεῖς, ὅτι αὐτοὶ κληρονομήσουσι τὴν γῆν.

Διδαχή.

vii. 1. βαπτίσατε εἰς τὸ ὄνομα τοῦ πατρὸς καὶ τοῦ υἱοῦ καὶ τοῦ ἁγίου πνεύματος.

viii. 2. μηδὲ προσεύχεσθε ὡς οἱ ὑποκριταί, ἀλλ᾽ . . . οὕτω προσεύχεσθε· Πάτερ ἡμῶν ὁ ἐν τῷ οὐρανῷ, ἁγιασθήτω τὸ ὄνομά σου, ἐλθέτω ἡ βασιλεία σου, γενηθήτω τὸ θέλημά σου, ὡς ἐν οὐρανῷ καὶ ἐπὶ γῆς· τὸν ἄρτον ἡμῶν τὸν ἐπιούσιον δὸς ἡμῖν σήμερον καὶ ἄφες ἡμῖν τὴν ὀφειλὴν ἡμῶν ὡς καὶ ἡμεῖς ἀφίεμεν τοῖς ὀφειλέταις ἡμῶν, καὶ μὴ εἰσενέγκῃς ἡμᾶς εἰς πειρασμόν, ἀλλὰ ῥῦσαι ἡμᾶς ἀπὸ τοῦ πονηροῦ· ὅτι σοῦ ἐστιν ἡ δύναμις καὶ ἡ δόξα εἰς τοὺς αἰῶνας.

x. 5. σύναξον [τὴν ἐκκλησίαν] ἀπὸ τῶν τεσσάρων ἀνέμων.

ix. 5. Μη δῶτε τὸ ἅγιον τοῖς κυσί.

x. 5. βασιλείαν, ἣν ἡτοίμασας αὐτῇ.

Scripture.

Matt. xxviii. 19. βαπτίσαντες αὐτοὺς εἰς τὸ ὄνομα τοῦ πατρὸς καὶ τοῦ υἱοῦ καὶ τοῦ ἁγίου πνεύματος.

Matt. vi. 5. ὅταν προσεύχησθε, οὐκ ἔσεσθε ὡς οἱ ὑποκριταί. 9—13: οὕτως οὖν προσεύχεσθε ὑμεῖς· Πάτερ ἡμῶν ὁ ἐν τοῖς οὐρανοῖς· ἁγιασθήτω τὸ ὄνομά σου, ἐλθέτω ἡ βασιλεία σου, γενηθήτω τὸ θέλημα σου, ὡς ἐν οὐρανῷ καὶ ἐπὶ τῆς γῆς· τὸν ἄρτον ἡμῶν τὸν ἐπιούσιον δὸς ἡμῖν σήμερον· καὶ ἄφες ἡμῖν τὰ ὀφειλήματα ἡμῶν, ὡς καὶ ἡμεῖς ἀφίεμεν τοῖς ὀφειλέταις ἡμῶν· καὶ μὴ εἰσενέγκῃς ἡμᾶς εἰς πειρασμόν, ἀλλὰ ῥῦσαι ἡμᾶς ἀπὸ τοῦ πονηροῦ· ὅτι σοῦ ἐστιν ἡ βασιλεία καὶ ἡ δύναμις καὶ ἡ δόξα εἰς τοὺς αἰῶνας. Ἀμήν.

Matt. xxiv. 31 : ἐπισυνάξουσι τοὺς ἐκλεκτοὺς αὐτοῦ ἐκ τῶν τεσσάρων ἀνέμων.

Matt. vii. 6. μὴ δῶτε τὸ ἅγιον τοῖς κυσί.

Matt. xxv. 34. τὴν ἡτοιμασμένην ὑμῖν βασιλείαν.

Διδαχή.	Scripture.

Διδαχή.

x. 6. ὡσαννὰ τῷ θεῷ Δαβιδ.

Matt. xxi. 9, 15. ὡσαννὰ τῷ υἱῷ Δαβίδ.

xi. 7. πᾶσα γὰρ ἁμαρτία ἀφεθήσεται, αὕτη δὲ ἁμαρτία οὐκ ἀφεθήσεται.

Matt xii. 31. πᾶσα ἁμαρτία . . . ἀφεθήσεται τοῖς ἀνθρώποις, ἡ δὲ τοῦ πνεύματος βλασφημία οὐκ ἀφεθήσεται.

xiii. 1, 2. προφήτης (διδάσκαλος) ἄξιος ὥσπερ ἐργάτης τῆς τροφῆς αὐτοῦ.

Matt. x. 10. ἄξιος γὰρ ὁ ἐργάτης τῆς τροφῆς αὐτοῦ.

xiv. 2. Πᾶς δὲ ἔχων ἀμφιβολίαν μετὰ τοῦ ἑταίρου αὐτοῦ μὴ συνελθέτω ὑμῖν, ἕως οὗ διαλλαγῶσιν, ἵνα μὴ κοινωθῇ ἡ θυσία ὑμῶν.

Matt. v. 23, 24. ἐὰν οὖν προσφέρῃς τὸ δῶρόν σου ἐπὶ τὸ θυσιαστήριον . . ὕπαγε, πρῶτον διαλλάγηθι τῷ ἀδελφῷ σου . . . καὶ τότε πρόσφερε τὸ δῶρόν σου.

xvi. 1. Γρηγορεῖτε ὑπερ τῆς ζωῆς ὑμῶν· οἱ λύχνοι ὑμῶν μὴ σβεσθήτωσαν, καὶ αἱ ὀσφύες ὑμῶν μὴ ἐκλυέσθωσαν, ἀλλὰ γίνεσθε ἕτοιμοι· οὐ γὰρ οἴδατε τὴν ὥραν, ἐν ᾗ ὁ κύριος ἡμῶν ἔρχεται.

Matt. xxiv. 42, 44. γρηγορεῖτε οὖν ὅτι οὐκ οἴδατε ποίᾳ ἡμέρᾳ ὁ κύριος ὑμῶν ἔρχεται . . . γίνεσθε ἕτοιμοι, ὅτι ᾗ οὐ δοκεῖτε ὥρᾳ ὁ υἱὸς τοῦ ἀνθρώπου ἔρχεται. Luke xii. 35. ἔστωσαν ὑμῶν αἱ ὀσφύες περιεζωσμέναι καὶ οἱ λύχνοι καιόμενοι.

xvi. 3, 4. Ἐν γὰρ ταῖς ἐσχάταις ἡμέραις πληθυνθήσονται οἱ ψευδοπροφῆται καὶ οἱ φθορεῖς καὶ στραφή-

Matt. xxiv. 10, 11. καὶ ἀλλήλους παραδώσουσιν καὶ μισήσουσιν ἀλλήλους· καὶ πολλοὶ ψευδοπροφῆται

Διδαχή.

σονται τὰ πρόβατα εἰς λύ-
κους καὶ ἡ ἀγάπη στρα-
φήσεται εἰς μῖσος· αὐξα-
νούσης γὰρ τῆς ἀνομίας,
μισήσουσιν ἀλλήλους καὶ
διώξουσι καὶ παραδώσουσι.
xvi. 5. καὶ σκανδαλισθήσονται πολλοὶ καὶ ἀπολοῦν-
ται, οἱ δὲ ὑπομείναντες ἐν
τῇ πίστει αὐτῶν σωθήσον-
ται.
xvi. 6—8. καὶ τότε φανή-
σεται τὰ σημεῖα τῆς ἀλη-
θείας· πρῶτον, σημεῖον ἐκπετάσεως ἐν οὐρανῷ, εἶτα
σημεῖον φωνῆς σάλπιγγος
καὶ τὸ τρίτον ἀνάστασις
νεκρῶν, οὐ πάντων δέ...
τότε ὄψεται ὁ κόσμος τὸν
κύριον ἐρχόμενον ἐπάνω
τῶν νεφελῶν τοῦ οὐρανοῦ.

Scripture.

ἐγερθήσονται καὶ πλανή-
σουσιν πολλούς· καὶ διὰ
τὸ πληθυνθῆναι τὴν ἀνο-
μίαν ψυγήσεται ἡ ἀγάπη
τῶν πολλῶν.

Matt. xxiv. 10, 13. καὶ
τότε σκανδαλισθήσονται
πολλοὶ... ὁ δὲ ὑπομεί-
νας εἰς τέλος οὗτος σωθή-
σεται.

Matt. xxiv. 20, 31. καὶ
τότε φανήσεται τὸ σημεῖον
τοῦ υἱοῦ τοῦ ἀνθρώπου ἐν
οὐρανῷ... καὶ ὄψονται
τὸν υἱὸν τοῦ ἀνθρώπου ἐρ-
χόμενον ἐπὶ τῶν νεφελῶν
τοῦ οὐρανοῦ... καὶ ἀπο-
στελεῖ τοὺς ἀγγέλους αὐ-
τοῦ μετὰ σάλπιγγος μεγά-
λης καὶ ἐπισυνάξουσιν τοῖς
ἐκλεκτοὺς αὐτοῦ.

INDEX TO PASSAGES OF SCRIPTURE.

C

THE EPISTLE OF BARNABAS, AND THE
SHEPHERD OF HERMAS.

THE writings of the Apostolical Fathers are sufficiently well known and accessible to render it unnecessary for the Editor to say more here than that he considers

1. The Epistle of Barnabas to have been written by a Gentile Christian of Alexandria, at the end of the first century.

2. The Shepherd of Hermas to have been written by a Jewish, or at least Judaizing, Christian (very possibly by two authors with a slight interval), during the first half of the second century.

In the following extracts the words corresponding with the Διδαχή are printed in the smaller type, with the reference to the chapter and verse; the larger representing the additions made by Barnabas and Hermas.

Διδαχή.]

EPISTLE OF BARNABAS.

[I. 1] XVIII. Ὁδοὶ δύο εἰσὶ διδαχῆς καὶ ἐξουσίας, ἥ τε τοῦ φωτὸς καὶ ἡ τοῦ σκότους· διαφορὰ δὲ πολλὴ τῶν δύο ὁδῶν. Ἐφ' ἧς μὲν γάρ εἰσι τεταγμένοι φωταγωγοὶ ἄγγελοι τοῦ Θεοῦ, ἐφ' ἧς δὲ ἄγγελοι τοῦ σατανᾶ· καὶ ὁ μέν ἐστι κύριος ἀπ' αἰώνων καὶ εἰς τοὺς αἰῶνας, ὁ δὲ ἄρχων καιροῦ τοῦ νῦν τῆς ἀνομίας.

[2] XIX. Ἀγαπήσεις τόν σε ποιήσαντα, φοβηθήσῃ τόν σε πλάσαντα, δοξάσεις τόν σε λυτρωσάμενον ἐκ θανάτου. Ἔσῃ ἁπλοῦς τῇ καρδίᾳ καὶ πλούσιος τῷ πνεύ-

[IV. 12] ματι. Οὐ κολληθήσῃ μετὰ τῶν πορευομένων ἐν ὁδῷ

[13] θανάτου. Μισήσεις πᾶν ὃ οὐκ ἔστιν ἀρεστὸν τῷ Θεῷ, μισήσεις

[III. 9] πᾶσαν ὑπόκρισιν, οὐ μὴ ἐγκαταλίπῃς ἐντολὰς Κυρίου. Οὐχ

ὑψώσεις σεαυτόν, ἔσῃ δὲ ταπεινόφρων κατὰ πάντα, [Διδαχή.]
οὐκ ἀρεῖς ἐπὶ σεαυτὸν δόξαν. Οὐ λήψῃ βουλὴν πονη- [II. 6]
ρὰν κατὰ τοῦ πλησίον σου. Οὐ δώσεις τῇ ψυχῇ σου θράσος. [III. 9]
Οὐ πορνεύσεις, οὐ μοιχεύσεις, οὐ παιδοφθορήσεις. Οὐ μή [II. 2]
σου ὁ λόγος τοῦ Θεοῦ ἐξέλθῃ ἐν ἀκαθαρσίᾳ τινῶν.
Οὐ λήψῃ πρόσωπον ἐλέγξαι τινὰ ἐπὶ παραπτώματι. Ἔσῃ [IV. 3]
πραΰς, ἔσῃ ἡσύχιος, ἔσῃ τρέμων τοὺς λόγους οὓς ἤκουσας. [III. 7, 8]
Οὐ μνησικακήσεις τῷ ἀδελφῷσου. Οὐ μὴ διψυχήσῃς, πό- [II. 3]
τερον ἔσται ἢ οὔ. Οὐ μὴ λάβῃς ἐπὶ ματαίῳ τὸ ὄνομα [IV. 4]
Κυρίου. Ἀγαπήσεις τὸν πλησίον σου ὑπὲρ τὴν ψυχήν σου. [II. 7]
Οὐ φονεύσεις τέκνον ἐν φθορᾷ, οὐδὲ πάλιν γεννηθὲν ἀπο- [II. 2]
κτενεῖς. Οὐ μὴ ἄρῃς τὴν χεῖρά σου ἀπὸ τοῦ υἱοῦ σου ἢ ἀπὸ [IV. 9]
τῆς θυγατρός σου, ἀλλ᾽ ἀπὸ νεότητος διδάξεις φόβον Κυρίου.
Οὐ μὴ γένῃ ἐπιθυμῶν τὰ τοῦ πλησίον σου, οὐ μὴ γένῃ πλεο- [II. 2]
νέκτης, οὐδὲ κολληθήσῃ ἐκ ψυχῆς σου μετὰ ὑψηλῶν, ἀλλὰ [II. 6]
μετὰ ταπεινῶν καὶ δικαίων ἀναστραφήσῃ. Τὰ συμβαίνοντά [III. 9]
σοι ἐνεργήματα ὡς ἀγαθὰ προσδέξῃ, εἰδὼς ὅτι ἄνευ Θεοῦ [10]
οὐδὲν γίνεται. Οὐκ ἔσῃ διγνώμων οὐδὲ δίγλωσσος· παγὶς [II. 4]
γὰρ θανάτου ἐστὶν ἡ διγλωσσία. Ὑποταγήσῃ κυρίοις ὡς [IV. 11]
τύπῳ Θεοῦ ἐν αἰσχύνῃ καὶ φόβῳ· οὐ μὴ ἐπιτάξῃς δούλῳ σου [10]
ἢ παιδίσκῃ σου ἐν πικρίᾳ τοῖς ἐπὶ τὸν αὐτὸν Θεὸν ἐλπίζουσι,
μή ποτε οὐ φοβηθῶσι τὸν ἐπ᾽ ἀμφοτέροις Θεόν· ὅτι ἦλθεν οὐ
κατὰ πρόσωπον καλέσαι, ἀλλ᾽ ἐφ᾽ οὓς τὸ πνεῦμα ἡτοίμασε.
Κοινωνήσεις ἐν πᾶσι τῷ πλησίον σου καὶ οὐκ ἐρεῖς ἴδια εἶναι· [8]
εἰ γὰρ ἐν τῷ ἀφθάρτῳ κοινωνοί ἐστε, πόσῳ μᾶλλον ἐν τοῖς
φθαρτοῖς; Οὐκ ἔσῃ πρόγλωσσος· παγὶς γὰρ στόμα
θανάτου. Ὅσον δύνασαι ὑπὲρ τῆς ψυχῆς σου
ἁγνεύσεις. Μὴ γίνου πρὸς μὲν τὸ λαβεῖν ἐκτείνων τὰς [5]
χεῖρας, πρὸς δὲ τὸ δοῦναι συσπῶν. Ἀγαπήσεις ὡς κόρην
τοῦ ὀφθαλμοῦ σου πάντα τὸν λαλοῦντά σοι τὸν λόγον [1]
τοῦ Κυρίου. Μνησθήσῃ ἡμέραν κρίσεως ἡμέρας καὶ νυκτὸς [2]

[Διδαχή.] καὶ ἐκζητήσεις καθ᾽ ἑκάστην ἡμέραν τὰ πρόσωπα τῶν ἁγίων,
ἢ διὰ λόγου κοπιῶν καὶ πορευόμενος εἰς τὸ παρα-
[6] καλέσαι καὶ μελετῶν εἰς τὸ σῶσαι ψυχὴν τῷ λόγῳ
[7] ἢ διὰ τῶν χειρῶν σου ἐργάσῃ εἰς λύτρον ἁμαρτιῶν σου. Οὐ
διστάσεις δοῦναι, οὐδὲ διδοὺς γογγύσεις· γνώσῃ δὲ τίς ὁ τοῦ
[13] μισθοῦ καλὸς ἀνταποδότης. Φυλάξεις ἃ παρέλαβες, μήτε προστιθεὶς μήτε ἀφαιρῶν. Εἰς τέλος μισήσεις τὸ πονηρόν.
[IV. 3] Κρινεῖς δικαίως. Οὐ ποιήσεις σχίσμα, εἰρηνεύσεις δὲ μαχο-
[14] μένους συναγαγών. Ἐξομολογήσῃ ἐπὶ ἁμαρτίᾳ σου, οὐ
προσήξεις ἐπὶ προσευχὴν ἐν συνειδήσει πονηρᾷ. Αὕτη ἐστὶν
ἡ ὁδὸς τοῦ φωτός.

[V. 1]   XX. Ἡ δὲ τοῦ μέλανος ὁδὸς σκολιά ἐστι καὶ κατάρας
μεστή· ὁδὸς γάρ ἐστι θανάτου αἰωνίου μετὰ τιμωρίας, ἐν ᾗ
ἐστι τὰ ἀπολλύντα τὴν ψυχὴν αὐτῶν εἰδωλολατρεία,
θρασύτης, ὕψος δυνάμεως, ὑπόκρισις, διπλοκαρδία, μοιχεία, φόνος, ἁρπαγή, ὑπερηφανία, παράβασις, δόλος, κακία, αὐθά-
[2] δεια, φαρμακεία, μαγεία, πλεονεξία, ἀφοβία Θεοῦ· διῶκται
τῶν ἀγαθῶν, μισοῦντες ἀλήθειαν, ἀγαπῶντες ψεῦδος, οὐ γινώσκοντες μισθὸν δικαιοσύνης, οὐ κολλώμενοι ἀγαθῷ οὐ κρίσει
δικαίᾳ, χήρᾳ καὶ ὀρφανῷ οὐ προσέχοντες, ἀγρυπνοῦντες
οὐκ εἰς φόβον Θεοῦ, ἀλλ᾽ ἐπὶ τὸ πονηρόν, ὧν μακρὰν καὶ
πόρρω πραΰτης καὶ ὑπομονή· ἀγαπῶντες μάταια, διώκοντες
ἀνταπόδομα, οὐκ ἐλεοῦντες πτωχόν, οὐ πονοῦντες ἐπὶ καταπονουμένῳ, εὐχερεῖς ἐπὶ καταλαλιᾷ, οὐ γινώσκοντες τὸν
ποιήσαντα αὐτούς, φονεῖς τέκνων, φθορεῖς πλάσματος Θεοῦ,
ἀποστρεφόμενοι τὸν ἐνδεόμενον, καταπονοῦντες τὸν θλιβόμενον,
πλουσίων παράκλητοι, πενήτων ἄνομοι κριταί, πανθαμάρτητοι.

[XVI. 2]   IV. Διὸ προσέχωμεν ἐν ταῖς ἐσχάταις ἡμέραις·
οὐδὲν γὰρ ὠφελήσει ἡμᾶς ὁ πᾶς χρόνος τῆς ζωῆς ἡμῶν καὶ τῆς
πίστεως, ἐὰν μὴ νῦν ἐν τῷ ἀνόμῳ καιρῷ καὶ τοῖς μέλλουσι
σκανδάλοις, ὡς πρέπει υἱοῖς Θεοῦ, ἀντιστῶμεν.

HERMAE PASTOR. MANDATUM II.

Ἐργάζου τὸ ἀγαθὸν καὶ ἐκ τῶν κόπων σου, ὧν [Διδαχή
ὁ Θεὸς δίδωσί σοι, πᾶσιν ὑστερουμένοις δίδου
ἁπλῶς, μὴ διστάζων τίνι δῷς ἢ τίνι μὴ δῷς· πᾶσι [I. 5]
δίδου· πᾶσι γὰρ ὁ Θεὸς δίδοσθαι θέλει ἐκ τῶν ἰδίων δωρη-
μάτων. Οἱ οὖν λαμβάνοντες ἀποδώσουσι λόγον τῷ Θεῷ διὰ
τί ἔλαβον καὶ εἰς τί· οἱ μὲν γὰρ λαμβάνοντες θλιβόμενοι οὐ
δικασθήσονται, οἱ δὲ ἐν ὑποκρίσει λαμβάνοντες τίσουσι δίκην.
Ὁ οὖν διδοὺς ἀθῷός ἐστιν· ὡς γὰρ ἔλαβε παρὰ Κυρίου
τὴν διακονίαν τελέσαι ἁπλῶς αὐτὴν ἐτέλεσε, μηδὲν
διακρίνων τίνι δῷ ἢ μὴ δῷ.

VI. 2. Ὅρα νῦν καὶ τοῦ ἀγγέλου τῆς πονηρίας [V. 1]
τὰ ἔργα. Πρῶτον πάντων . . . τὰ ἔργα αὐτοῦ πονηρά . . . ὅτι ἡ διδαχὴ αὐτοῦ πονηρά ἐστι.

XI. Οὕτω δοκιμάσεις τὸν προφήτην καὶ τὸν ψευ- [XI.]
δοπροφήτην· ἀπὸ τῆς ζωῆς δοκίμαζε τὸν ἄνθρωπον
τὸν ἔχοντα τὸ πνεῦμα τὸ θεῖον. Πρῶτον μὲν ὁ
ἔχων τὸ πνεῦμα τὸ θεῖον, τὸ ἄνωθεν, πραΰς ἐστι
καὶ ἡσύχιος καὶ ταπεινόφρων καὶ ἀπεχόμενος ἀπὸ
πάσης πονηρίας καὶ ἐπιθυμίας ματαίας τοῦ αἰῶνος
τούτου καὶ ἑαυτὸν ἐνδεέστερον ποιεῖ πάντων τῶν
ἀνθρώπων . . . [ὁ ψευδοπροφήτης] μισθοὺς λαμβάνει τῆς προφητείας αὐτοῦ, ἐὰν δὲ μὴ λάβῃ, οὐ
προφητεύει. Δύναται οὖν πνεῦμα θεῖον μισθοὺς
λαμβάνειν καὶ προφητεύειν ; Οὐκ ἐνδέχεται τοῦτο
ποιεῖν Θεοῦ προφήτην, ἀλλὰ τῶν τοιούτων προφητῶν ἐπίγειόν ἐστι τὸ πνεῦμα. . . . Ἔχεις ἀμ-
φοτέρων τῶν προφητῶν τὴν ζωήν. Δοκίμαζε οὖν
ἀπὸ τῶν ἔργων καὶ τῆς ζωῆς τὸν ἄνθρωπον τὸν
λέγοντα ἑαυτὸν πνευματοφόρον εἶναι.

ILLUSTRATIONS, No. III.

FROM AN EARLY LATIN TRANSLATION OF A PORTION OF THE Διδαχή[a].

In the Library of a Benedictine Abbey at Mölk, in Austria, there seems to have existed, according to a notice published at Vienna in 1747, a MS. of the ninth or tenth century, in which, amongst other writings, was contained, on the last page, a Latin treatise, "Doctrina Apostolorum," but, as is added, in an imperfect condition.

Von Gebhardt, whose attention was roused by this notice, at once commenced enquiries. The MS. at present cannot be found, but Bernard Pez, Librarian of the Abbey in the last century, published as much as existed of the MS. in the Second Part of the Fourth Volume of his *Thesaurus Anecdotorum Novissimus*, p. 5. It is unfortunately only a very short fragment.

Immediately at the end of a Sermon of St. Boniface follow the words:—

"*Tum in Codice post perbrevia quædam S. Augustini dicta comparet* Doctrina Apostolorum, *eadem, qua Sermo S.Bonifacii, manu exarata, quæ sic habet.*"

[a] From a notice communicated by v. Gebhardt to Harnack's edition of the Διδαχή, in *Texte und Untersuchungen*, vol. ii. pt. 2, Leipzig, 1884.

DOCTRINA APOSTOLORUM.

[Chap. I.ᵇ]

[1.] Viæ duæ sunt *in seculo*, vitæ et mortis, *lucis et tenebrarum. In his constituti sunt Angeli duo, unus æquitatis alter iniquitatis.* Distantia autem magna est duarum viarum.

[2.] Via ergo vitæ hæc est : Primò diliges Deum *æternum*, qui te fecit. Secundò proximum tuum, ut te ipsum. Omne autem, quod tibi non vis fieri, alii ne feceris.

[3.] Interpretatio autem horum verborum hæc est.

  ✦   •   •   •   •

[Chap. II.]

[2.] Non mæchaberis, non homicidium facies, non falsum testimonium dices, non puerum violaveris, non fornicaveris. . . . Non medicamenta mala facies ; non occides filium in abortum, nec natum succides. Non concupisces quidquam de re proximi tui.

[3.] Non perjurabis. Non male loqueris. Non eris memor malorum factorum.

[4.] Non eris duplex in consilium dandum, neque bilinguis ; tendiculum ᶜ enim mortis est lingua.

[5.] Non erit verbum tuum vacuum nec mendax.

[6.] Non eris cupidus nec avarus, nec rapax, nec adulator nec . . .

 ᵇ The chapters and verses in brackets refer to the chapters and paragraphs of the Διδαχή.

 ᶜ The neuter *tendiculum*, instead of *tendicula*, has no authority given by Forcellini, except two passages in writings of Vigilius, Bp. of Thapsus.

The first difference between the Latin translation and the Greek original to be noted is in the title, but if the translator lived when the title "Apostles" was confined to the twelve, he would be not unlikely to omit the number. The second title is also omitted for whatever reason.

There are some slight additions, shewn above by the use of italic type, "in seculo," "lucis et tenebrarum," and the following sentence, "In his constituti—tenebrarum," I. 1. The latter two seem to be taken from the Epistle of Barnabas, xviii. 1. In *v.* 2, "æternum" is also added.

In ch. ii. verse 2, it will be observed that the first two sentences are transposed, non falsum testimonium dices is brought from verse 3, and the words οὐ κλέψεις, οὐ μαγεύσεις are omitted altogether.

Besides variations by additions, the Latin text is marked by the omission of the passage from the word εὐλογεῖτε, I. 3, to τῆς διδαχῆς, II. 1; for the list of sins, so far as the translation goes, seems to make it clear that the Latin writer had the genuine Διδαχή before him. It is a singular fact that the same passage is wanting in the Egyptian "Ecclesiastical Canons;" while it appears, though somewhat modified, in the Seventh Book of the Ap. Constitutions. Possibly the omission is due to accident on the part of the translator, but probably the passage was wanting in some copies of the Διδαχή.

ILLUSTRATIONS, No. IV.

EXTRACT FROM "THE ECCLESIASTICAL CANONS OF THE HOLY APOSTLES."

THERE exists in parts of Egypt, besides the "Constitutions of the Apostles," a collection of ecclesiastical law, the foundation of which agrees very closely with parts of the "Teaching of the Apostles." This collection goes by various names, such as the "Canons of the Apostles," the "Epitome of the Definitions of the Holy Apostles," &c. There is still much work for critics in investigating these writings, which are also extant in Syriac.

The reader has here before him Harnack's Greek Text, for comparison with that of the Διδαχή. It has been noticed, as a singular coincidence, that the passage, ch. i. 3 to ii. 2, which is wanting in this treatise, is also omitted in the Latin fragment of a translation of the Διδαχή.

It may be interesting, in the case of a work so little known, to summarize here Harnack's remarks on this body of rules, the received German title for which is *Apostolische Kirchen-Ordnung*.

In 1691, Ludolf published a Commentary on his History of Ethiopia, at Frankfort, in which he printed the original and a Latin version of a body of Ethiopian Canons, with the title, "Isti sunt Canones patrum Apostolorum quos constituerunt ad ordinandam ecclesiam Christianam." At the head, on p. 314, stand the canons we are now considering.

Next, A.D. 1711, Grabe, "Essay upon two Arabic
MSS., in the Bodleian Library," replying to Whiston,
who asserted that he had found in these MSS. very
early Christian teaching, in fact the Διδαχή, makes it
appear that Whiston had not seen the MSS., and
that "this Arabick Doctrine, except the Preface and
five or six leaves, is . . . the very first five entire
Books of [the Clementine Constitutions], and part of
the sixth" (Grabe, p. 11). Consequently these are
not the Canons we are dealing with *.

From this date they fall into oblivion, till Bickell
(*Geschichte des Kirchenrechts*, vol. i.), 1843, really in-
vestigated them critically and historically, and published the Vienna MS., giving the treatise the name
Apostolische Kirchen-Ordnung, which it now is known
by in Germany. A large part of this MS. contains the
usual oriental collection of canons, such as are found
worked up in the Apostolical Constitutions. In his
remarks Bickell gives proof of great critical sagacity
by declaring his conviction that neither the Epistle
of Barnabas, nor the "Apostolical Constitutions," were
the source of the work he was editing, but that there
must have been some third writing, more or less re-
lated to the Epistle of Barnabas, and probably known
to the compilers of *Const. Apost.*, bk. vii., and of this
work.

Five years later, A.D. 1848, Archdeacon Tattam,
from a modern Memphitic (i.e. North Egyptian) MS.
now numbered *Orient.*, 440, in the British Museum,
published the Coptic version, and an English trans-

---

* Harnack must have misunderstood the position of Grabe
and Whiston, if he had seen the Essay of the former.

lation of these Canons (see later, p. 34). There is
said to be an Arabic version in the same MS. Tattam
had also another more perfect MS. in the Thebaic or
Sahidic dialect of Upper Egypt, which Harnack says
is now in the Royal Library at Berlin; and Bishop
Lightfoot (Clement of Rome, App., p. 273, and 466),
speaking of these versions, refers to another older
Thebaic MS. of A.D. 1006, also in the British Museum,
Orient. 1320, from which version the Memphitic was
translated.

The next writer, in 1856, Lagarde, in his *Reliquiæ
Juris Ecclesiastici Antiquissimæ*, makes further progress by using a Syrian MS.[b] (Paris, *Cod. Sangerm.
Syr.* 38), described by Cureton, *Corpus Ignat.*, p. 342 f.
Book iii. in this collection has our treatise, but only
chapters iii. — xiii., apparently not an accidental de-
fect. Lagarde also refers to this MS. in Bunsen's *Ana-
lecta Ante Nicæna*, ii. 37 ff.

In 1864 Cardinal Pitra printed these canons in the
first volume of his *Juris Ecclesiastici Monumenta*, published at Rome, using the Vienna MS., and a fresh one
(*Ottobon. gr.*, 408) of the fourteenth century, in which,
under the title ἐπιτομὴ ὅρων τῶν ἁγίων ἀποστόλων καθο-
λικῆς παραδόσεως, exactly the same passages and omis-
sions exist as in the Syrian MS. used by Lagarde,
with a closing chapter peculiar to itself. *Cod. Ottob.*
is altogether shorter than *Cod. Vindob.* (the Vienna
MS.).

Two years after this Hilgenfeld (*Nov. Test. extra
Canon. recept.*, fasc. iv. pp. 93—106,—in the new
edition, p. 110) brought out the same work, making

[b] Published by Lagarde in his *Egyptiaca*, 1883.

use of the published editions. He contended that this
was the treatise spoken of by Rufinus as *Duæ viæ vel
Judicium Petri*, and by St. Jerome as *Petri Judicium*,
but he does not seem to have convinced any one.

There was again an interval, this time of twelve
years, till, in 1878, von Gebhardt and Harnack, in
their edition of Barnabas, took up Bickell's view,
using a fresh MS. of the tenth century, noticed by
von Gebhardt in the Library of the Holy Synod at
Moscow (*Cod. gr.* cxxv. Sæc. x.). This is the oldest
yet found, and, with some considerable variations, it
corresponds with c. 4—14, of the *Apostolische Kirchen-
Ordnung*. Its title is ἐκ τῶν διατάξεων τῶν ἁγίων ἀποστόλων. These Editors came to the conclusion that there
must have been some source of this work belonging
to the second century, which St. Clement of Alexandria and its compiler had used.

A marvellous product of ingenious critical skill was
an article by Krawutsky, in the *Tübinger Quartal Schrift*,
1882, pt. iii., in which he conjecturally reconstructed
what he believed must have been the original foundation of this body of rules; for his conjectures have
been proved, by the discovery of the Διδαχή, to have
been to a very great extent correct.

And, lastly, Bryennius has compared the Canons and
Διδαχή together, printing the Canons, and marking the
differences by change of type.

This body of ordinances or canons still, in spite of
its extreme antiquity, forms part of the Canon Law of
Egyptian Christians, and is therefore interesting in itself,
as well as in its relation to the Διδαχή, from which so
much of it is borrowed. Here and there a few slight

additions are made, mostly unimportant. It should have a distinct title of its own, and possibly no better one could be found than that of Lagarde, *Canones Ecclesiastici*, "Ecclesiastical Canons." This agrees with the Greek Κανόνες ἐκκλησιαστικοί, with the German *Kirchen-Ordnung* fairly well; and is sufficiently distinct from the titles, "Apostolical Canons," and "Apostolical Constitutions."

The parts of the following extracts which agree with the Διδαχή have the chapter and verse added in brackets at the side, and the small type is used when the language follows very closely that of the Διδαχή.

ΚΑΝΟΝΕΣ ΕΚΚΛΗΣΙΑΣΤΙΚΟΙ ΤΩΝ ΑΓΙΩΝ ΑΠΟΣΤΟΛΩΝ.

Χαίρετε, υἱοὶ καὶ θυγατέρες, ἐν ὀνόματι κυρίου Ἰησοῦ Χριστοῦ. Ἰωάννης καὶ Ματθαῖος καὶ Πέτρος καὶ Ἀνδρέας καὶ Φίλιππος καὶ Σίμων καὶ Ἰάκωβος καὶ Ναθαναὴλ καὶ Θωμᾶς καὶ Κηφᾶς καὶ Βαρθολομαῖος καὶ Ἰούδας Ἰακώβου.

1. Κατὰ κέλευσιν τοῦ κυρίου ἡμῶν Ἰησοῦ Χριστοῦ τοῦ σωτῆρος συναθροισθέντων ἡμῶν, καθὼς διέταξεν πρὸ τοῦ· Μέλλετε κληροῦσθαι τὰς ἐπαρχίας, καταλογίσασθαι τόπων ἀριθμούς, ἐπισκόπων ἀξίας, πρεσβυτέρων ἕδρας, διακόνων παρεδρείας, ἀναγνωστῶν νουνεχίας, χηρῶν ἀνεγκλησίας καὶ ὅσα δέοι πρὸς θεμελίωσιν ἐκκλησίας, ἵνα τύπον τῶν ἐπουρανίων εἰδότες φυλάσσωνται ἀπὸ παντὸς ἀστοχήματος, εἰδότες ὅτι λόγον ὑφέξουσιν ἐν τῇ

μεγάλῃ ἡμέρᾳ τῆς κρίσεως περὶ ὧν ἀκούσαντες
οὐκ ἐφύλαξαν—καὶ ἐκέλευσεν ἡμᾶς ἐκπέμψασθαι
τοὺς λόγους εἰς ὅλην τὴν οἰκουμένην·

2. ἔδοξεν οὖν ἡμῖν πρὸς ὑπόμνησιν τῆς ἀδελφό-
τητος καὶ νουθεσίαν ἑκάστῳ ὡς ὁ κύριος ἀπεκάλυψε
κατὰ τὸ θέλημα τοῦ θεοῦ διὰ πνεύματος ἁγίου
μνησθεῖσι λόγου ἐντείλασθαι ὑμῖν.

3. Ἰωάννης εἶπεν· ἄνδρες ἀδελφοί, εἰδότες ὅτι
λόγον ὑφέξομεν περὶ τῶν διατεταγμένων ἡμῖν εἰς
ἑνὸς πρόσωπον μὴ λαμβάνωμεν, ἀλλ᾽ ἐάν τις δοκῇ
τι ἀσύμφορον λέγειν, ἀντιλεγέσθω αὐτῷ. ἔδοξε δὲ
πᾶσι πρῶτον Ἰωάννην εἰπεῖν.

[I. 1.]   4. Ἰωάννης εἶπεν· ὁδοὶ δύο εἰσί, μία τῆς ζωῆς καὶ μία
[2]   τοῦ θανάτου, διαφορὰ δὲ πολλὴ μεταξὺ τῶν δύο ὁδῶν· ἡ μὲν
οὖν ὁδὸς τῆς ζωῆς ἐστιν αὕτη· πρῶτον· ἀγαπήσεις τὸν θεὸν
τὸν ποιήσαντά σε ἐξ ὅλης τῆς καρδίας σου καὶ δοξάσεις τὸν λυτρωσάμενόν σε ἐκ θανάτου, ἥτις ἐστὶν
[2] ἐντολὴ πρώτη. δεύτερον· ἀγαπήσεις τὸν πλησίον σου
ὡς ἑαυτόν, ἥτις ἐστὶν ἐντολὴ δευτέρα, ἐν οἷς ὅλος ὁ
νόμος κρέμαται καὶ οἱ προφῆται.

[2]   5. Ματθαῖος εἶπεν· πάντα ὅσα ἂν μὴ θέλῃς σοι γίνεσ-
θαι, μηδὲ σὺ ἄλλῳ ποιήσῃς. τούτων δὲ τῶν λόγων τὴν
διδαχὴν εἰπέ, ἀδελφὲ Πέτρε.

[II. 2]   6. Πέτρος εἶπεν· οὐ φονεύσεις, οὐ μοιχεύσεις, οὐ
πορνεύσεις, οὐ παιδοφθορήσεις, οὐ κλέψεις, οὐ μαγεύσεις,
οὐ φαρμακεύσεις, οὐ φονεύσεις τέκνον ἐν φθορᾷ οὐδὲ γεννηθὲν
[3] ἀποκτενεῖς, οὐκ ἐπιθυμήσεις τὰ τοῦ πλησίον· οὐκ ἐπιορκήσεις,
οὐ ψευδομαρτυρήσεις, οὐ κακολογήσεις, οὐδὲ μνησικακήσεις,
[4] οὐκ ἔσῃ δίγνωμος οὐδὲ δίγλωσσος· παγὶς γὰρ θανάτου ἐστὶν
[5] ἡ διγλωσσία. οὐκ ἔσται ὁ λόγος σου κενός, οὐδὲ ψευδής· οὐκ

ἔσῃ πλεονέκτης οὐδὲ ἅρπαξ οὐδὲ ὑποκριτὴς οὐδὲ κακοήθης [6]
οὐδὲ ὑπερήφανος, οὐ λήψῃ βουλὴν πονηρὰν κατὰ τοῦ πλησίον σου· οὐ μισήσεις πάντα ἄνθρωπον, ἀλλ᾽ οὓς μὲν ἐλέγξεις, [7]
οὓς δὲ ἐλεήσεις, περί ὧν δὲ προσεύξῃ, οὓς δὲ ἀγαπήσεις
ὑπὲρ τὴν ψυχήν σου.

7. Ἀνδρέας εἶπεν· τέκνον μου, φεῦγε ἀπὸ παντὸς [III. 1]
πονηροῦ καὶ ἀπὸ παντὸς ὁμοίου αὐτοῦ. μὴ γίνου ὀργίλος· [2]
ὁδηγεῖ γὰρ ἡ ὀργὴ πρὸς τὸν φόνον· ἔστι γὰρ δαιμόνιον
ἀρρενικὸν ὁ θυμός. μὴ γίνου ζηλωτὴς μηδὲ ἐριστικὸς μηδὲ [2]
θυμώδης· ἐκ γὰρ τούτων φόνος γεννᾶται.

8. Φίλιππος εἶπεν· τέκνον μου, μὴ γίνου ἐπιθυμητής· [3]
ὁδηγεῖ γὰρ ἡ ἐπιθυμία πρὸς τὴν πορνείαν καὶ ἕλκει τοὺς
ἀνθρώπους πρὸς ἑαυτήν. ἔστι γὰρ θηλυκὸν δαιμόνιον ἡ ἐπιθυμία, καὶ ὃ μὲν μετ᾽ ὀργῆς, ὃ δὲ μεθ᾽
ἡδονῆς ἀπόλλυσι τοὺς εἰσερχομένους εἰς αὐτήν.
ὁδὸς δὲ πονηροῦ πνεύματος ἁμαρτία ψυχῆς, καὶ
ὅταν βραχεῖαν εἴσδυσιν σχῇ ἐν αὐτῷ, πλατύνει
αὐτὴν καὶ ἄγει ἐπὶ πάντα τὰ κακὰ τὴν ψυχὴν
ἐκείνην καὶ οὐκ ἐᾷ διαβλέψαι τὸν ἄνθρωπον καὶ
ἰδεῖν τὴν ἀλήθειαν. ὁ θυμὸς ὑμῶν μέτρον ἐχέτω
καὶ ἐν βραχεῖ διαστήματι αὐτὸν ἡνιοχεῖτε καὶ ἀνα-
κρούετε, ἵνα μὴ ἐμβάλλῃ ὑμᾶς εἰς ἔργον πονηρόν.
θυμὸς γὰρ καὶ ἡδονὴ πονηρὰ ἐπὶ πολὺ παραμέ-
νοντα κατὰ ἐπίτασιν δαιμόνια γίνεται, καὶ ὅταν
ἐπιτρέψῃ αὐτοῖς ὁ ἄνθρωπος, οἰδαίνουσιν ἐν τῇ
ψυχῇ αὐτοῦ καὶ γίνονται μείζονες καὶ ἀπάγουσιν
αὐτὸν εἰς ἔργα ἄδικα καὶ ἐπιγελῶσιν αὐτῷ καὶ
ἥδονται ἐπὶ τῇ ἀπωλείᾳ τοῦ ἀνθρώπου.

9. Σίμων εἶπεν· τέκνον, μὴ γίνου αἰσχρολόγος μηδὲ [3]
ὑψηλόφθαλμος· ἐκ γὰρ τούτων μοιχεία γεννᾶται.

[4]   10. Ἰάκωβος εἶπεν· τέκνον μου, μὴ γίνου οἰωνοσκόπος,
ἐπειδὴ ὁδηγεῖ εἰς τὴν εἰδωλολατρίαν, μηδὲ ἐπαοιδὸς μηδὲ
μαθηματικὸς μηδὲ περικαθαίρων μηδὲ θέλε αὐτὰ ἰδεῖν μηδὲ
ἀκούειν. ἐκ γὰρ τούτων ἁπάντων εἰδωλολατρίαι γεννῶνται.

[5]   11. Ναθαναὴλ εἶπεν· τέκνον, μὴ γίνου ψεύστης,
ἐπειδὴ ὁδηγεῖ· τὸ ψεῦσμα ἐπὶ τὴν κλοπήν, μηδὲ φιλάργυρος
μηδὲ κενόδοξος. ἐκ γὰρ τούτων ἁπάντων κλοπαὶ γεννῶνται.

[6] τέκνον, μὴ γίνου γόγγυσος, ἐπειδὴ ἄγει πρὸς τὴν βλασφημίαν,
μηδὲ αὐθάδης μηδὲ πονηρόφρων. ἐκ γὰρ τούτων ἁπάντων
[7] βλασφημίαι γεννῶνται. ἴσθι δὲ πραΰς, ἐπεὶ πραεῖς κληρονο-
[8] μήσουσι τὴν βασιλείαν τῶν οὐρανῶν. γίνου μακρόθυμος,
ἐλεήμων, εἰρηνοποιός, καθαρὸς τῇ καρδίᾳ ἀπὸ παντὸς
κακοῦ, ἄκακος καὶ ἡσύχιος, ἀγαθὸς καὶ φυλάσσων καὶ
[9] τρέμων τοὺς λόγους οὓς ἤκουσας· οὐχ ὑψώσεις σεαυτὸν οὐδὲ
δώσεις τὴν ψυχήν σου μετὰ ὑψηλῶν, ἀλλὰ μετὰ δικαίων καὶ
ταπεινῶν ἀναστραφήσῃ. τὰ δὲ συμβαίνοντά σοι ἐνεργήματα
ὡς ἀγαθὰ προσδέξῃ, εἰδὼς ὅτι ἄτερ Θεοῦ οὐδὲν γίνεται.

[IV. 1]   12. Θωμᾶς εἶπεν· τέκνον, τὸν λαλοῦντά σοι τὸν λόγον
τοῦ Θεοῦ καὶ παραίτιόν σοι γινόμενον τῆς ζωῆς καὶ
δόντα σοι τὴν ἐν Κυρίῳ σφραγῖδα ἀγαπήσεις ὡς
κόρην ὀφθαλμοῦ σου, μνησθήσῃ δὲ αὐτοῦ νύκτα καὶ
ἡμέραν, τιμήσεις αὐτὸν ὡς τὸν Κύριον. ὅθεν γὰρ ἡ κυριότης
[2] λαλεῖται, ἐκεῖ Κύριός ἐστιν. ἐκζητήσεις δὲ τὸ πρόσωπον αὐτοῦ
καθ᾽ ἡμέραν καὶ τοὺς λοιποὺς ἁγίους, ἵνα ἐπαναπαύσῃ
τοῖς λόγοις αὐτῶν· κολλώμενος γὰρ ἁγίοις ἁγιασθήσῃ.
τιμήσεις δὲ αὐτόν, καθ᾽ ὃ δυνατὸς εἶ, ἐκ τοῦ ἱδρῶτός
σου καὶ ἐκ τοῦ πόνου τῶν χειρῶν σου. εἰ γὰρ ὁ
Κύριος δι᾽ αὐτοῦ ἠξίωσέν σοι δοθῆναι πνευματικὴν
τροφὴν καὶ ποτὸν καὶ ζωὴν αἰώνιον, σὺ ὀφείλεις
πολὺ μᾶλλον τὴν φθαρτὴν καὶ πρόσκαιρον προσφέ-

ρειν τροφήν· ἄξιος γὰρ ὁ ἐργάτης τοῦ μισθοῦ αὐτοῦ, καὶ
βοῦν ἀλοῶντα οὐ φιμώσεις, καὶ οὐδεὶς φυτεύει ἀμ-
πελῶνα καὶ ἐκ τοῦ καρποῦ αὐτοῦ οὐκ ἐσθίει.

13. Κηφᾶς εἶπεν· οὐ ποιήσεις σχίσματα, εἰρηνεύσεις [3]
δὲ μαχομένους. κρινεῖς δικαίως, οὐ λήψῃ πρόσωπον ἐλέγξαι
τινὰ ἐπὶ παραπτώματι. οὐ γὰρ ἰσχύει πλοῦτος παρὰ
Κυρίῳ· οὐ γὰρ ἀξία προκρίνει οὐδὲ κάλλος ὠφελεῖ,
ἀλλ' ἰσότης ἐστὶ πάντων παρ' αὐτῷ. ἐν προσευχῇ
σου μὴ διψυχήσῃς πότερον ἔσται ἢ οὔ· μὴ γίνου πρὸς μὲν τὸ [4, 5]
λαβεῖν ἐκτείνων τὰς χεῖρας, πρὸς δὲ τὸ δοῦναι συσπῶν. ἐὰν [6]
ἔχῃς διὰ τῶν χειρῶν σου, δώσεις λύτρωσιν τῶν ἁμαρτιῶν σου.
οὐ διστάσεις δοῦναι οὐδὲ διδοὺς γογγύσεις· γνώσῃ γάρ, τίς [7]
ἐστιν ὁ τοῦ μισθοῦ καλὸς ἀνταποδότης. οὐκ ἀποστραφήσῃ [8]
ἐνδεόμενον, συγκοινωνήσεις δὲ πάντα τῷ ἀδελφῷ σου καὶ οὐκ
ἐρεῖς ἴδια εἶναι· εἰ γὰρ ἐν τῷ ἀθανάτῳ κοινωνοί ἐστε, πόσῳ
μᾶλλον ἐν τοῖς θνητοῖς.

ILLUSTRATIONS, No. V.

The following translation of the Ecclesiastical Canons is taken from a work entitled "The Apostolical Constitutions or Canons of the Apostles in Coptic, with an English Translation by Henry Tattam," &c.—London, 1848. It is also given in Bunsen's "Hippolytus and his Age," vol. iii. p. 9, English translation.

Bishop Lightfoot speaks of the original as "not made directly from the Greek, but a very recent and somewhat barbarous translation from the previously Thebaic version." St. Clement of Rome, App., p. 273, and p. 466.

[I. 1] 4. JOHN said, "There are two ways, one is the way
[2] of life, and the other is the way of death: and there is much difference in these two ways. But the way of life is this, Thou shalt love the Lord thy God with all thy heart, who created thee, and thou shalt glorify Him who redeemed thee from death; for this is the first Commandment.

[2] But the second is this, Thou shalt love thy neighbour as thyself. On these two Commandments hang the Law and the Prophets."

[2] 5. Matthew said, "Every thing that thou wouldest not should be done to thee, that do not thou also to another; that is, what thou hatest do not to another.

[a] An account of this has already been given on p. 26.

But thou, O Peter my brother, teach them these things."

6. Peter said, "Thou shalt not kill; thou shalt not [II. 2] commit adultery; thou shalt not commit fornication; thou shalt not pollute a youth; thou shalt not steal; thou shalt not be a sorcerer; thou shalt not use divination; thou shalt not cause a woman to miscarry, neither if she has brought forth a child shalt thou kill it; thou shalt not covet any thing that is thy neighbour's; thou shalt not bear false witness; thou shalt [3] not speak evil of any one, neither shalt thou think evil; thou shalt not be double-minded, neither shalt [4] thou be double-tongued, for a double tongue is a snare of death; thy speech shall not be vain, neither [5] tending to a lie; thou shalt not be covetous, neither [6] rapacious, nor an hypocrite, nor of an evil heart, nor proud; thou shalt not speak an evil word against thy neighbour; thou shalt not hate any man, but thou shalt reprove some, and shalt have mercy upon others; thou shalt pray for some, and shalt love others as thy own soul."

7. Andrew said, "My son, flee from all evil, and [III. 1] hate all evil. Be not angry, because anger leads to [2] murder, for anger is an evil demon. Be not emulous, neither be contentious, nor quarrelsome, for envy proceeds from these."

8. Philip said, "My son, be not of unlawful desires, [3] because desire leads to fornication, drawing men to it involuntarily; for lust is a demon. For if the evil spirit of anger is united with that of lust, they destroy those who shall receive them. And the way of the evil spirit is the sin of the soul. For when he

sces a little quiet [? way], entering in he will make the
way broad; and he will take with him all other evil
spirits: he will go to that soul and will not leave
the man to meditate at all, lest he should see the truth.
Let a restraint be put upon your anger, and curb it
with not a little care, that you may cast it behind you,
lest it should precipitate you into some evil deed.
For wrath and evil desire, if they be suffered always
to remain, are demons. And when they have dominion
over a man they change him in soul, that he may be
prepared for a great deed: and when they have led
him into unrighteous acts, they deride him, and will
rejoice in the destruction of that man."

[3]   9. Simon said, "My son, be not the utterer of an evil
expression, nor of obscenity, neither be thou haughty,
for of these things come adulteries."

[4]   10. James said, "My son, be not a diviner, for divination leadeth to idolatry; neither be thou an en-
chanter, nor an astrologer, nor a magician, nor an
idolater, [*Sahidic*, one that bewitcheth]; neither teach
them nor hear them; for from these things proceedeth
idolatry." ·

[5]   11. Nathanael said, "My son, be not a liar, because
a falsehood leadeth to blasphemy. Neither be thou
a lover of silver nor a lover of vainglory, for from these
thefts arise.

[6]   "My son, be not a murmurer, because repining
leads a man to blasphemy. Be thou not harsh, nor
a thinker of evil, for of all these things contentions
[7] are begotten. But be thou meek, for the meek shall
[8] inherit the earth. And be thou also merciful, peace-
able, compassionate, cleansed in thy heart from all

evil. Be thou sincere, gentle, good; trembling at the words of God, which thou hast heard, and do thou keep them. Do not exalt thyself, neither shalt thou [9] give thy heart to pride, but thou shalt increase more and more with the just and humble. Every evil which cometh upon thee receive as good, knowing that nothing shall come upon thee but from God."

12. Thomas said, "My son, he who declares to [IV. 1] thee the words of God, and hath been the cause of life to thee, and hath given to thee the holy seal which is in the Lord, thou shalt love him as the apple of thine eyes, and remember him by night and day: thou shalt honour him as of the Lord: for in that place in which the word of power is, there is the Lord; and thou shalt seek his face daily, him, and those who [2] remain of the saints, that thou mayest rest thee on their words: for he who is united to the saints shall be holy.

"Thou shalt honour him according to thy power, by the sweat of thy brow, and by the labour of thy hands: for if the Lord hath made thee meet that He might impart to thee spiritual food, and spiritual drink, and eternal life, by him; it becomes thee also the more, that thou shouldest impart to him the food which perishes and is temporal; for the labourer is worthy of his hire. For it is written: Thou shalt not muzzle the ox treading out the corn; neither does any one plant a vineyard and not eat of the fruit thereof."

13. Cephas said, "Thou shalt not make schisms: [3] thou shalt reconcile in peace those who contend with one another. Judge in righteousness without accept-

ing of persons. Reprove him who hath sinned, for
his sin. Suffer not wealth to prevail before God,
neither justify the unworthy, for beauty profiteth
[4] not; but righteous judgment before all. Doubt not
in thy prayer, thinking whether what thou hast asked
[5] of Him will be or not. Let it not, indeed, be, that
when thou receivest thou stretchest out thine hand,
but when thou shouldest give thou drawest thy hand
[6] to thee. But if thou hast at hand, thou shalt give
[7] for the redemption of thy sins. Thou shalt not doubt,
thou shalt give; neither when thou hast given shalt
[8] thou murmur, knowing this reward is of God. Thou
shalt not turn away from the needy, but shalt com-
[8] municate with the needy in all things : thou shalt not
say, these things are mine alone. If ye communicate
with one another in those things which are incorrup-
tible, how much rather should ye not do it in those
things which are corruptible."

14. Bartholomew said, "I beseech you, my brethren,
while you have time, and he who asks remains with
you, and you are able to do good to them, do not fail
in any thing to any one, which you have the power
to do.

[XVI.]   "For the Day of the Lord draweth nigh, in which
every thing that is seen shall be dissolved, and the
wicked shall be destroyed with it; for the Lord cometh, and His reward is with Him.

"Be ye lawgivers to your own selves; be ye teachers
[IV. 3] to yourselves alone, as God hath taught you. Thou
shalt keep those things which thou hast received; thou
shalt not take from them, neither shalt thou add to
them."

ILLUSTRATIONS, No. VI.

THE APOSTOLICAL CONSTITUTIONS.

THE eight books of the Apostolical Constitutions contain rules for laity and clergy, compiled probably from three sources, of which a writing similar to the Διδαχή is the foundation of Book vii., and is probably not without influence in other portions. The compilation probably dates from the middle of the third for the earliest, to the middle of the fourth century, for the later portions.

The Quinisext, or Council in Trullo (A.D. 680), at Constantinople, in its second Canon, while admitting the Apostolic Canons, rejects the διατάξεις, or Constitutions, as marred by heretical interpolation, but at the same time implies that they contain much worthy of acceptance.

The portion given here in illustration is that in which the Διδαχή is, to a large extent, imbedded, as is shewn by the use of smaller type in the following pages.

CONSTITUTIONES APOSTOLICÆ, VII. 1—32.[a]

1. Τοῦ νομοθέτου Μωσέως εἰρηκότος τοῖς Ἰσραηλίταις· Ἰδοὺ δέδωκα πρὸ προσώπου ὑμῶν τὴν ὁδὸν τῆς ζωῆς καὶ τὴν ὁδὸν τοῦ θανάτου, καὶ ἐπιφέροντος· Ἔκλεξαι τὴν ζωὴν ἵνα ζήσῃς· καὶ τοῦ προφήτου Ἠλία λέγοντος τῷ λαῷ· Ἕως πότε χω-

[a] The references in brackets at the side are to the chapters and verses of the Διδαχή.

λανεῖτε ἐπ᾽ ἀμφοτέραις ταῖς ἰγνύαις ὑμῶν; εἰ
Θεός ἐστι Κύριος, πορεύεσθε ὀπίσω αὐτοῦ, εἰκότως
ἔλεγε καὶ ὁ Κύριος Ἰησοῦς· Οὐδεὶς δύναται δυσὶ
κυρίοις δουλεύειν· ἢ γὰρ τὸν ἕνα μισήσει καὶ
τὸν ἕτερον ἀγαπήσει, ἢ ἑνὸς ἀνθέξεται καὶ τοῦ
ἑτέρου καταφρονήσει, ἀναγκαίως καὶ ἡμεῖς ἑπό-
μενοι τῷ διδασκάλῳ Χριστῷ, ὅς ἐστι σωτὴρ πάντων ἀνθρώπων μάλιστα πιστῶν, φαμὲν ὡς δύο
[I. 1] ὁδοί εἰσι, μία τῆς ζωῆς καὶ μία τοῦ θανάτου. Οὐδεμίαν
δὲ σύγκρισιν ἔχουσι πρὸς ἑαυτάς (πολὺ γὰρ τὸ
διάφορον), μᾶλλον δὲ πάντη κεχωρισμέναι τυγχά-
νουσι, καὶ φυσικὴ μὲν ἐστιν ἡ τῆς ζωῆς ὁδός,
ἐπείσακτος δὲ ἡ τοῦ θανάτου, οὐ τοῦ κατὰ γνώμην
θεοῦ ὑπάρξαντος, ἀλλὰ τοῦ ἐξ ἐπιβουλῆς τοῦ ἀλ-
[2] λοτρίου. Πρώτη οὖν τυγχάνει ἡ ὁδὸς τῆς ζωῆς· Καὶ
ἔστιν αὕτη, ἣν καὶ ὁ νόμος διαγορεύει, ἀγαπᾶν Κύριον
τὸν Θεὸν ἐξ ὅλης τῆς καρδίας καὶ ἐξ ὅλης τῆς ψυχῆς
[2] τὸν ἕνα καὶ μόνον, παρ᾽ ὃν ἄλλος οὐκ ἔστι, καὶ τὸν
πλησίον ὡς ἑαυτόν. Καὶ πᾶν ὃ μὴ θέλεις γενέσθαι σοι, καὶ
[3] σὺ τοῦτο ἄλλῳ οὐ ποιήσεις. Εὐλογεῖτε τοὺς καταρωμένους
ὑμᾶς, προσεύχεσθε ὑπὲρ τῶν ἐπηρεαζόντων ὑμᾶς, ἀγαπᾶτε
τοὺς ἐχθροὺς ὑμῶν. Ποία γὰρ ὑμῖν χάρις, ἐὰν φιλῆτε
τοὺς φιλοῦντας ὑμᾶς; καὶ γὰρ οἱ ἐθνικοὶ τοῦτο ποιοῦσιν·
ὑμεῖς δὲ φιλεῖτε τοὺς μισοῦντας ὑμᾶς καὶ ἐχθρὸν οὐχ ἕξετε·
οὐ μισήσεις γάρ, φησί, πάντα ἄνθρωπον, οὐκ
Αἰγύπτιον, οὐκ Ἰδουμαῖον, ἅπαντες γάρ εἰσιν
τοῦ θεοῦ ἔργα. Φεύγετε δὲ οὐ τὰς φύσεις, ἀλλὰ
[4] τὰς γνώμας τῶν κακῶν. Ἀπέχου τῶν σαρκικῶν καὶ
κοσμικῶν ἐπιθυμιῶν. Ἐάν τις σοι δῷ ῥάπισμα εἰς τὴν
δεξιὰν σιαγόνα, στρέψον αὐτῷ καὶ τὴν ἄλλην· οὐ φαύλης

οὔσης τῆς ἀμύνης, ἀλλὰ τιμιωτέρας τῆς ἀνεξικα-
κίας· λέγει γὰρ ὁ Δαβίδ· Εἰ ἀνταπέδωκα τοῖς
ἀνταποδιδοῦσί μοι κακά. Ἐὰν ἀγγαρεύσῃ σε τὶς
μίλιον ἕν, ὕπαγε μετ' αὐτοῦ δύο, καὶ τῷ θέλοντί σοι
κριθῆναι καὶ τὸν χιτῶνά σου λαβεῖν, ἄφες αὐτῷ καὶ τὸ
ἱμάτιον, καὶ ἀπὸ τοῦ αἴροντος τὰ σὰ μὴ ἀπαίτει. Τῷ [ʊ]
αἰτοῦντί σε δίδου, καὶ ἀπὸ τοῦ θέλοντος δανείσασθαι
παρὰ σοῦ μὴ (ἀποστραφεὶς) ἀποκλείσῃς τὴν χεῖρα,
δίκαιος γὰρ ἀνὴρ οἰκτείρει καὶ κιχρᾷ· πᾶσι γὰρ [ʊ]
θέλει δίδοσθαι ὁ Πατὴρ ὁ τὸν ἥλιον αὐτοῦ ἀνατέλλων
ἐπὶ πονηροὺς καὶ ἀγαθούς, καὶ τὸν ὑετὸν αὐτοῦ
βρέχων ἐπὶ δικαίους καὶ ἀδίκους. Πᾶσιν οὖν δίκαιον
διδόναι ἐξ οἰκείων πόνων· τίμα γάρ, φησί, τὸν Κύριον
ἀπὸ σῶν δικαίων πόνων· προτιμητέον δὲ τοὺς
ἁγίους.

2. Οὐ φονεύσεις, τοῦτ' ἔστιν οὐ φθερεῖς τὸν ὅμοιόν [II. 2]
σοι ἄνθρωπον· διαλύεις γὰρ τὰ καλῶς γενόμενα·
οὐχ ὡς παντὸς φόνου φαύλου τυγχάνοντος, ἀλλὰ
μόνου τοῦ ἀθώου, τοῦ δὲ ἐνδίκου ἄρχουσι μόνοις
ἀφωρισμένου. Οὐ μοιχεύσεις, διαιρεῖς γὰρ τὴν μίαν [2]
σάρκα εἰς δύο· Ἔσονται γάρ, φησίν, οἱ δύο εἰς
σάρκα μίαν· ἐν γάρ εἰσιν ἀνὴρ καὶ γυνὴ τῇ φύσει,
τῇ συμπνοίᾳ, τῇ ἑνώσει, τῇ διαθέσει, τῷ βίῳ, τῷ
τρόπῳ, κεχωρισμένοι δέ εἰσι τῷ σχήματι καὶ τῷ
ἀριθμῷ. Οὐ παιδοφθορήσεις· παρὰ φύσιν γὰρ τὸ [2]
κακὸν ἐκ Σοδόμων φυέν, ἥτις πυρὸς θεηλάτου
παρανάλωμα γέγονεν· ἐπικατάρατος δὲ ὁ τοιοῦτος
καὶ ἐρεῖ πᾶς ὁ λαός· Γένοιτο. Οὐ πορνεύσεις· οὐκ [2]
ἔσται γάρ, φησί, πορνεύων ἐν υἱοῖς Ἰσραήλ. Οὐ [2]
κλέψεις· Ἄχαρ γὰρ κλέψας ἐν τῷ Ἰσραὴλ ἐν

Ἱεριχὼ λίθοις βληθεὶς τοῦ ζῆν ὑπεξῆλθε, καὶ
Γιεζεῖ κλέψας καὶ ψευσάμενος ἐκληρονόμησε τοῦ
Νεεμὰν τὴν λέπραν, καὶ Ἰούδας κλέπτων τὰ τῶν
πενήτων τὸν Κύριον τῆς δόξης παρέδωκεν Ἰου-
δαίοις, καὶ μεταμεληθεὶς ἀπήγξατο καὶ ἐλάκησε
μέσος καὶ ἐξεχύθη πάντα τὰ σπλάγχνα αὐτοῦ, καὶ
Ἀνανίας καὶ Σαπφείρα ἡ τούτου γυνή, κλέψαντες
τὰ ἴδια καὶ πειράσαντες τὸ Πνεῦμα Κυρίου, παρα-
χρῆμα ἀποφάσει Πέτρου τοῦ συναποστόλου ἡμῶν
ἐθανατώθησαν.

[II. 2]   3. Οὐ μαγεύσεις, οὐ φαρμακεύσεις· φαρμακοὺς γάρ,
[2] φησίν, οὐ περιβιώσετε.   Οὐ φονεύσεις τέκνον ἐν φθορᾷ
οὐδὲ τὸ γεννηθὲν ἀποκτενεῖς· πᾶν γὰρ τὸ ἐξεικονισμένον,
ψυχὴν λαβὸν παρὰ θεοῦ, φονευθὲν ἐκδικηθήσεται,
[2] ἀδίκως ἀναιρεθέν.   Οὐκ ἐπιθυμήσεις τὰ τοῦ πλησίον σου,
οἷον τὴν γυναῖκα ἢ τὸν παῖδα ἢ τὸν βοῦν ἢ τὸν
[3] ἀγρόν.   Οὐκ ἐπιορκήσεις· ἐρρήθη γὰρ μὴ ὀμόσαι ὅλως·
εἰ δὲ μή γε, κἂν εὐορκήσῃς, ὅτι ἐπαινεθήσεται πᾶς
[3] ὁ ὀμνύων ἐν αὐτῷ.   Οὐ ψευδομαρτυρήσεις, ὅτι ὁ συ-
κοφαντῶν πένητα παροξύνει τὸν ποιήσαντα αὐτόν.

[3]   4. Οὐ κακολογήσεις· Μὴ ἀγάπα γάρ, φησί, κακο-
[3] λογεῖν, ἵνα μὴ ἐξαρθῇς· οὐδὲ μνησικακήσεις· ὁδοὶ γὰρ
[4] μνησικάκων εἰς θάνατον.   Οὐκ ἔσῃ δίγνωμος οὐδὲ
δίγλωσσος· παγὶς γὰρ ἰσχυρὰ ἀνδρὶ τὰ ἴδια χείλη,
καὶ Ἀνὴρ γλωσσώδης οὐ κατευθυνθήσεται ἐπὶ τῆς
[5] γῆς· οὐκ ἔσται ὁ λόγος σου κενός· περὶ παντὸς γὰρ
λόγου ἀργοῦ δώσετε λόγον· οὐ ψεύσῃ· ἀπολεῖς γὰρ
[6] πάντας τοὺς λαλοῦντας τὸ ψεῦδος.   Οὐκ ἔσῃ πλεονέκτης οὐδὲ ἅρπαξ.   Οὐαὶ γάρ, φησίν, ὁ πλεονεκτῶν

τὸν πλησίον πλεονεξίαν κακήν. Οὐκ ἔσῃ ὑποκριτής, [II. 6]
ἵνα μὴ τὸ μέρος σου μετ' αὐτῶν θῇς.

5. Οὐκ ἔσῃ κακοήθης, οὐδὲ ὑπερήφανος· ὑπερηφάνοις [6]
γὰρ ὁ Θεὸς ἀντιτάσσεται. Οὐ λήψῃ πρόσωπον
δυνάστου ἐν κρίσει, τοῦ γὰρ Κυρίου ἡ κρίσις. Οὐ [7]
μισήσεις πάντα ἄνθρωπον· ἐλεγμῷ ἐλέγξεις τὸν ἀδελφόν σου
καὶ οὐ λήψῃ δι' αὐτὸν ἁμαρτίαν, καὶ "Ελεγχε
σοφὸν καὶ ἀγαπήσει σε. Φεῦγε ἀπὸ παντὸς κακοῦ καὶ [III. 1]
ἀπὸ παντὸς ὁμοίου αὐτῷ· "Απεχε γάρ, φησίν, ἀπὸ
ἀδίκου καὶ τρόμος οὐκ ἐγγιεῖ σοι. Μὴ γίνου ὀργίλος, [2]
μηδὲ βάσκανος, μηδὲ ζηλωτής, μηδὲ μανικός, μηδὲ
θρασύς, μὴ πάθῃς τὰ τοῦ Κάϊν καὶ τὰ τοῦ Σαοὺλ
καὶ τὰ τοῦ Ἰωάβ· ὅτι ὁ μὲν ἀπέκτεινε τὸν ἀδελ-
φὸν αὐτοῦ τὸν "Αβελ διὰ τὸ πρόκριτον αὐτὸν εὑρεθῆναι παρὰ θεῷ καὶ διὰ τὸ προκριθῆναι τὴν θυσίαν αὐτοῦ· ὃς δὲ τὸν ὅσιον Δαβὶδ ἐδίωκε νική-
σαντα Γολιὰθ τὸν Φυλιστιαῖον, καὶ ζηλώσας ἐπὶ
τῇ τῶν χορευτριῶν εὐφημίᾳ, ὃς δὲ τοὺς δύο στρα-
τηλάτας ἀνεῖλε, τὸν Ἀβενὴρ τὸν τοῦ Ἰσραὴλ καὶ
Ἀμεσσὰ τὸν τοῦ Ἰούδα.

6. Μὴ γίνου οἰωνοσκόπος, ὅτι ὁδηγεῖ πρὸς εἰδωλολατρείαν· [4]
Οἰώνισμα δέ, φησὶν ὁ Σαμουήλ, ἁμαρτία ἐστίν,
καὶ Οὐκ ἔσται οἰωνισμὸς ἐν Ἰακὼβ οὐδὲ μαντεία
ἐν Ἰσραήλ· οὐκ ἔσῃ ἐπάδων ἢ περικαθαίρων τὸν υἱόν σου, [4]
οὐ κληδονιεῖς οὐδὲ οἰωνισθήσῃ οὐδὲ ὀρνεοσκοπή-
σεις οὐδὲ μαθήσῃ μάθημα πονηρόν· ταῦτα γὰρ πάντα
καὶ ὁ νόμος ἀπεῖπεν. Μὴ γίνου ἐπιθυμητὴς κακῶν,
ὁδηγηθήσῃ γὰρ εἰς ἀμετρίαν ἁμαρτημάτων. Οὐκ
ἔσῃ αἰσχρολόγος οὐδὲ ῥιψόφθαλμος οὐδὲ μέθυσος· ἐκ γὰρ [3]
τούτων πορνεῖαι καὶ μοιχεῖαι γίνονται. Μὴ γίνου φιλάργυρος, [5]

[III. 5] ἵνα μὴ ἀντὶ Θεοῦ δουλεύσῃς τῷ μαμωνᾷ. Μὴ γίνου
κενόδοξος, μηδὲ μετέωρος, μηδὲ ὑψηλόφρων· ἐκ γὰρ
τούτων ἁπάντων ἀλαζονίαι γίνονται· μνήσθητι τοῦ εἰ-
πόντος, Κύριε, οὐχ ὑψώθη ἡ καρδία μου οὐδὲ ἐμε-
τεωρίσθησαν οἱ ὀφθαλμοί μου, οὐδὲ ἐπορεύθην
ἐν μεγάλοις οὐδὲ ἐν θαυμασίοις ὑπὲρ ἐμέ, εἰ μὴ
ἐταπεινοφρόνουν.

[6] 7. Μὴ γίνου γόγγυσος, μνησθεὶς τῆς τιμωρίας, ἧς
[6] ὑπέστησαν οἱ καταγογγύσαντες Μωσέως. Μὴ ἔσο
αὐθάδης μηδὲ πονηρόφρων μηδὲ σκληροκάρδιος μηδὲ
[6] θυμώδης μηδὲ μικρόψυχος· ταῦτα γὰρ πάντα ὁδηγεῖ
[7] πρὸς βλασφημίαν· ἴσθι δὲ πρᾶος ὡς Μωῦσῆς καὶ Δαβίδ,
ἐπεὶ οἱ πραεῖς κληρονομήσουσι τὴν γῆν.

[8] 8. Γίνου μακρόθυμος· ὁ γὰρ τοιοῦτος πολὺς ἐν
φρονήσει, ἐπείπερ ὁ ὀλιγόψυχος ἰσχυρὸς ἄφρων.
[8] Γίνου ἐλεήμων· μακάριοι γὰρ οἱ ἐλεήμονες, ὅτι αὐτοὶ
[8] ἐλεηθήσονται. Ἔσο ἄκακος, ἥσυχος, ἀγαθός, τρέμων
[9] τοὺς λόγους τοῦ θεοῦ. Οὐχ ὑψώσεις σεαυτὸν ὡς ὁ Φαρισ-
αῖος· ὅτι πᾶς ὁ ὑψῶν ἑαυτὸν ταπεινωθήσεται, καὶ
τὸ ὑψηλὸν ἐν ἀνθρώποις βδέλυγμα παρὰ θεῷ.
[9] Οὐ δώσεις τῇ ψυχῇ σου θράσος, ὅτι ἀνὴρ θρασὺς ἐμ-
πεσεῖται εἰς κακά. Οὐ συμπορεύσῃ μετὰ ἀφρό-
[10] νων, ἀλλὰ μετὰ σοφῶν καὶ δικαίων· Τὰ συμβαίνοντά
σοι πάθη εὐμενῶς δέχου καὶ τὰς περιστάσεις ἀλύ-
πως, εἰδὼς ὅτι μισθὸς παρὰ Θεοῦ σοι δοθήσεται
ὡς τῷ Ἰὼβ καὶ τῷ Λαζάρῳ.

[IV. 1] 9. Τὸν λαλοῦντά σοι τὸν λόγον τοῦ Θεοῦ δοξάσεις, μνησθήσῃ δὲ αὐτοῦ ἡμέρας καὶ νυκτός, τιμήσεις δὲ αὐτὸν οὐχ
ὡς γενέσεως αἴτιον, ἀλλ᾽ ὡς τοῦ εὖ εἶναί σοι πρό-
[1] ξενον γινόμενον· ὅπου γὰρ ἡ περὶ Θεοῦ διδασκαλία, ἐκεῖ

ὁ Θεὸς πάρεστιν. Ἐκζητήσεις καθ' ἡμέραν τὸ πρόσωπον τῶν [IV. 2]
ἁγίων, ἵν' ἐπαναπαύῃ τοῖς λόγοις αὐτῶν.

10. Οὐ ποιήσεις σχίσματα πρὸς τοὺς ἁγίους, μνησ- [3]
θεὶς τῶν Κορειτῶν. Εἰρηνεύσεις μαχομένους ὡς Μωσῆς [3]
συναλλάσσων εἰς φιλίαν. Κρινεῖς δικαίως· τοῦ γὰρ [3]
κυρίου ἡ κρίσις. Οὐ λήψῃ πρόσωπον ἐλέγξαι ἐπὶ πα- [3]
ραπτώματι, ὡς Ἠλίας καὶ Μιχαίας τὸν Ἀχαάβ,
καὶ Ἀβδεμέλεχ ὁ Αἰθίοψ τὸν Σεδεκίαν, καὶ
Νάθαν τὸν Δαβίδ, καὶ Ἰωάννης τὸν Ἡρώδην.

11. Μὴ γίνου δίψυχος ἐν προσευχῇ σοῦ, εἰ ἔσται ἢ [4]
οὔ· λέγει γὰρ ὁ κύριος ἐμοὶ Πέτρῳ ἐπὶ τῆς θα-
λάσσης· Ὀλιγόψυχε, εἰς τί ἐδίστασας; Μὴ γίνου [5]
πρὸς μὲν τὸ λαβεῖν ἐκτείνων τὴν χεῖρα, πρὸς δὲ τὸ δοῦναι
συστέλλων.

12. Ἐὰν ἔχῃς διὰ τῶν χειρῶν σου, δός, ἵνα ἐργάσῃ [6]
εἰς λύτρωσιν ἁμαρτιῶν σου· ἐλεημοσύναις γὰρ καὶ
πίστεσιν ἀποκαθαίρονται ἁμαρτίαι. Οὐ διστάσεις [7]
δοῦναι πτωχῷ, οὐδὲ διδοὺς γογγύσεις· γνώσῃ γὰρ τίς
ἐστιν ὁ τοῦ μισθοῦ ἀνταποδότης· Ὁ ἐλεῶν γάρ, φησί,
πτωχὸν Κυρίῳ δανείζει, κατὰ δὲ τὸ δόμα αὐτοῦ,
οὕτως ἀνταποδοθήσεται αὐτῷ. Οὐκ ἀποστραφήσῃ [8]
ἐνδεόμενον· ὃς φράσσει γάρ, φησί, τὰ ὦτα αὐτοῦ
μὴ ἀκοῦσαι ἐνδεομένου, καὶ αὐτὸς ἐπικαλέσεται
καὶ οὐκ ἔσται ὁ εἰσακούων αὐτοῦ. Κοινωνήσεις εἰς [8]
πάντα τῷ ἀδελφῷ σου καὶ οὐκ ἐρεῖς ἴδια εἶναι· κοινὴ γὰρ
ἡ μετάληψις παρὰ Θεοῦ πᾶσιν ἀνθρώποις παρε-
σκευάσθη. Οὐκ ἀρεῖς τὴν χεῖρά σου ἀπὸ τοῦ υἱοῦ σου ἢ [9]
ἀπὸ τῆς θυγατρός σου, ἀλλὰ ἀπὸ νεότητος διδάξεις αὐτοὺς
τὸν φόβον τοῦ Θεοῦ. Παίδευε γάρ, φησί, τὸν υἱόν
σου, οὕτω γὰρ ἔσται σοι εὔελπις.

[IV. 10] 13. Οὐκ ἐπιτάξεις δούλῳ σου ἢ παιδίσκῃ τοῖς ἐπὶ τὸν αὐτὸν Θεὸν πεποιθόσιν ἐν πικρίᾳ ψυχῆς, μή ποτε στενάξωσιν ἐπὶ σοὶ καὶ ἔσται σοι ὀργὴ παρὰ Θεοῦ· καὶ [11] ὑμεῖς, οἱ δοῦλοι, ὑποτάγητε τοῖς κυρίοις ὑμῶν ὡς τύπῳ Θεοῦ ἐν αἰσχύνῃ καὶ φόβῳ ὡς Κυρίῳ καὶ οὐκ ἀνθρώποις.

[12] 14. Μισήσεις πᾶσαν ὑπόκρισιν, καὶ πᾶν ὃ ἐὰν ᾖ ἀρεστὸν [13] Κυρίῳ, ποιήσεις· οὐ μὴ ἐγκαταλίπῃς ἐντολὰς Κυρίου, φυλάξεις δὲ ἃ παρέλαβες παρ᾽ αὐτοῦ, μήτε προστιθεὶς ἐπ᾽ αὐτοῖς μήτε ἀφαιρῶν ἀπ᾽ αὐτῶν· οὐ προσθήσεις γὰρ τοῖς λόγοις αὐτοῦ, ἵνα μὴ ἐλέγξῃ σε καὶ ψευδὴς γένῃ. [14] Ἐξομολογήσῃ Κυρίῳ τῷ Θεῷ σου τὰ ἁμαρτήματά σου καὶ οὐκέτι προσθήσεις ἐπ᾽ αὐτοῖς, ἵνα εὖ σοι γένηται παρὰ Κυρίῳ τῷ Θεῷ σου, ὃς οὐ βούλεται τὸν θάνατον τοῦ ἁμαρτωλοῦ, ἀλλὰ τὴν μετάνοιαν.

15. Τὸν πατέρα σου καὶ τὴν μητέρα θεραπεύσεις ὡς αἰτίους σοι γενέσεως, ἵνα γένῃ μακροχρόνιος ἐπὶ τῆς γῆς ἧς Κύριος ὁ Θεός σου δίδωσί σοι· τοὺς ἀδελφούς σου καὶ τοὺς συγγενεῖς σου μὴ ὑπερίδῃς· τοὺς γὰρ οἰκείους τοῦ σπέρματός σου οὐχ ὑπερόψει.

16. Τὸν βασιλέα φοβηθήσῃ, εἰδὼς ὅτι τοῦ Κυρίου ἐστὶν ἡ χειροτονία· τοὺς ἄρχοντας αὐτοῦ τιμήσεις ὡς λειτουργοὺς Θεοῦ, ἔκδικοι γάρ εἰσιν πάσης ἀδικίας· οἷς ἀποτίσατε τέλος, φόρον καὶ πᾶσαν εἰσφορὰν εὐγνωμόνως.

[14] 17. Οὐ προσελεύσῃ ἐπὶ προσευχήν σου ἐν ἡμέρᾳ πονηρίας σου, πρὶν ἂν λύσῃς τὴν πικρίαν σου. Αὕτη ἐστὶν ἡ ὁδὸς τῆς ζωῆς, ἧς γένοιτο ἐντὸς ὑμᾶς εὑρεθῆναι διὰ Ἰησοῦ Χριστοῦ τοῦ Κυρίου ἡμῶν.

18. Ἡ δὲ ὁδὸς τοῦ θανάτου ἐστὶν ἐν πράξεσι πονη- [V. 1]
ραῖς θεωρουμένη· ἐν αὐτῇ γὰρ ἄγνοια τοῦ Θεοῦ
καὶ πολλῶν θεῶν ἐπεισαγωγή, δι᾽ ὧν φόνοι, μοιχεῖαι,
πορνεῖαι, ἐπιορκίαι, ἐπιθυμίαι παράνομοι, κλοπαί, εἰδω-
λολατρεῖαι, μαγεῖαι, φαρμακεῖαι, ἁρπαγαί, ψευδομαρτυρίαι,
ὑποκρίσεις, διπλοκαρδία, δόλος, ὑπερηφανία, κακία, αὐθάδεια,
πλεονεξία, αἰσχρολογία, ζηλοτυπία, θρασύτης, ὑψηλοφρο-
σύνη, ἀλαζονεία, ἀφοβία, διωγμὸς ἀγαθῶν, ἀληθείας ἔχθρα, [2]
ψεύδους ἀγάπη, ἄγνοια δικαιοσύνης. Οἱ γὰρ τούτων ποιη-
ταὶ οὐ κολλῶνται ἀγαθῷ οὐδὲ κρίσει δικαίᾳ· ἀγρυπνοῦσιν [2]
οὐκ εἰς τὸ ἀγαθόν, ἀλλ᾽ εἰς τὸ πονηρόν· ὧν μακρὰν πραότης
καὶ ὑπομονή, μάταια ἀγαπῶντες, διώκοντες ἀνταπόδομα, οὐκ
ἐλεοῦντες πτωχόν, οὐ πονοῦντες ἐπὶ καταπονουμένῳ, οὐ γινώσκοντες τὸν ποιήσαντα αὐτούς, φονεῖς τέκνων, φθορεῖς
πλάσματος Θεοῦ, ἀποστρεφόμενοι ἐνδεόμενον, καταπονοῦντες
θλιβόμενον, πλουσίων παράκλητοι, πενήτων ὑπερόπται,
πανθαμάρτητοι. Ῥυσθείητε, τέκνα, ἀπὸ τούτων πάντων.

19. Ὅρα μή τίς σε πλανήσῃ ἀπὸ τῆς εὐσεβείας· Οὐκ [VI. 1]
ἐκκλινεῖς γάρ, φησίν, ἀπ᾽ αὐτῆς δεξιὰ ἢ ἀριστερά,
ἵνα συνῇς ἐν πᾶσιν οἷς ἐὰν πράσσῃς· σὺ γάρ, ἐὰν
ἐκτραπῇς τῆς εὐθείας ὁδοῦ, δυσσεβήσεις.

20. Περὶ δὲ βρωμάτων λέγει σοι ὁ Κύριος· Τὰ [3]
ἀγαθὰ τῆς γῆς φάγεσθε, καί, Πᾶν κρέα ἔδεσθε ὡς
λάχανα χλόης, τὸ δὲ αἷμα ἐκχεεῖς· οὐ γὰρ τὰ εἰσερ-
χόμενα εἰς τὸ στόμα κοινοῖ τὸν ἄνθρωπον, ἀλλὰ
τὰ ἐκπορευόμενα, λέγω δὴ βλασφημίαι, καταλαλιαὶ
καὶ εἴ τι τοιοῦτον. Σὺ δὲ φάγῃ τὸν μυελὸν τῆς
γῆς μετὰ δικαιοσύνης· ὅτι εἴ τι καλόν, αὐτοῦ, καὶ
εἴ τι ἀγαθόν, αὐτοῦ· σῖτος νεανίσκοις καὶ οἶνος
εὐωδιάζων παρθένοις· τίς γὰρ φάγεται ἢ τίς πίεται
πάρεξ αὐτοῦ;

[3]   21. Ἀπὸ δὲ τῶν εἰδωλοθύτων φεύγετε, ἐπὶ τιμῇ γὰρ δαιμόνων θύουσι αὐτά, ἐφ' ὕβρει δηλαδὴ τοῦ μόνου Θεοῦ, ὅπως μὴ γένησθε κοινωνοὶ δαιμόνων.

[VII. 1]   22. Περὶ δὲ βαπτίσματος, ὦ ἐπίσκοπε ἢ πρεσβύτερε, ἤδη μὲν καὶ πρότερον διεταξάμεθα, καὶ νῦν
[1] δέ φαμεν ὅτι οὕτως βαπτίσεις, ὡς ὁ Κύριος διετάξατο ἡμῖν λέγων· Πορευθέντες μαθητεύσατε πάντα τὰ
[1] ἔθνη, βαπτίζοντες αὐτοὺς εἰς τὸ ὄνομα τοῦ Πατρὸς καὶ τοῦ Υἱοῦ καὶ τοῦ ἁγίου Πνεύματος, διδάσκοντες αὐτοὺς τηρεῖν πάντα ὅσα ἐνετειλάμην ὑμῖν· τοῦ ἀποστείλαντος Πατρός, μοῦ ἐλθόντος Χριστοῦ, τοῦ μαρτυρήσαντος Παρακλήτου. Χρίσεις δὲ πρῶτον ἐλαίῳ ἁγίῳ, ἔπειτα βαπτίσεις ὕδατι καὶ τελευταῖον σφραγίσεις μύρῳ· ἵνα τὸ μὲν χρίσμα μετοχὴ ᾖ τοῦ ἁγίου Πνεύματος, τὸ δὲ ὕδωρ σύμβολον τοῦ θανάτου, τὸ δὲ μύρον σφραγὶς τῶν συνθηκῶν. Εἰ δὲ μήτε ἔλαιον ᾖ μήτε μύρον, ἀρκεῖ τὸ ὕδωρ καὶ πρὸς χρίσιν καὶ πρὸς σφαγῖδα καὶ πρὸς ὁμολογίαν τοῦ
[1] ἀποθανόντος ἤτοι συναποθνήσκοντος. Πρὸ δὲ τοῦ βαπτίσματος νηστευσάτω ὁ βαπτιζόμενος· καὶ γὰρ ὁ Κύριος, ὑπὸ Ἰωάννου πρῶτον βαπτισθεὶς καὶ εἰς τὴν ἔρημον αὐλισθείς, μετέπειτα ἐνήστευσε τεσσαράκοντα ἡμέρας καὶ τεσσαράκοντα νύκτας. Ἐβαπτίσθη δὲ καὶ ἐνήστευσεν, οὐκ αὐτὸς ἀπορυπώσεως ἢ νηστείας χρείαν ἔχων ἢ καθάρσεως ὁ τῇ φύσει καθαρὸς καὶ ἅγιος, ἀλλ' ἵνα καὶ Ἰωάννῃ ἀλήθειαν προσμαρτυρήσῃ καὶ ἡμῖν ὑπογραμμὸν παράσχηται. Οὐκοῦν ὁ μὲν Κύριος οὐκ εἰς ἑαυτοῦ πάθος ἐβαπτίσατο ἢ θάνατον ἢ ἀνάστασιν (οὐδέπω γὰρ οὐδὲν τούτων ἐγεγόνει), ἀλλ' εἰς διάταξιν

ἑτέραν, διὸ καὶ ἀπ᾽ ἐξουσίας μετὰ τὸ βάπτισμα
νηστεύει ὡς Κύριος Ἰωάννου· ὁ δὲ εἰς τὸν αὐτοῦ
θάνατον μυούμενος πρότερον ὀφείλει νηστεῦσαι
καὶ τότε βαπτισθῆναι (οὐ γὰρ δίκαιον τὸν συν-
ταφέντα καὶ συναναστάντα παρ᾽ αὐτὴν τὴν ἀνάστασιν κατηφεῖν), οὐ γὰρ κύριος ὁ ἄνθρωπος τῆς
διατάξεως τῆς τοῦ Σωτῆρος· ἐπείπερ ὁ μὲν δεσ-
πότης, ὁ δὲ ὑπήκοος.

23. Αἱ δὲ νηστεῖαι ὑμῶν μὴ ἔστωσαν μετὰ τῶν ὑποκριτῶν, [VIII. 1]
νηστεύουσι γὰρ δευτέρᾳ σαββάτων καὶ πέμπτῃ. Ὑμεῖς δὲ
ἢ τὰς πέντε νηστεύσατε ἡμέρας, ἢ τετράδα καὶ παρα-
σκευήν· ὅτι τῇ μὲν τετράδι ἡ κρίσις ἐξῆλθεν ἡ κατὰ
τοῦ Κυρίου, Ἰούδα χρήμασιν ἐπαγγειλαμένου τὴν
προδοσίαν· τῇ δὲ παρασκευῇ, ὅτι ἔπαθεν ὁ Κύριος ἐν
αὐτῇ πάθος τὸ διὰ σταυροῦ ὑπὸ Ποντίου Πιλάτου.
Τὸ σάββατον μέντοι καὶ τὴν κυριακὴν ἑορτάζετε,
ὅτι τὸ μὲν δημιουργίας ἐστὶν ὑπόμνημα, τὸ δὲ
ἀναστάσεως. Ἐν δὲ μόνον σάββατον ὑμῖν φυ-
λακτέον ἐν ὅλῳ τῷ ἐνιαυτῷ, τὸ τῆς τοῦ Κυρίου
ταφῆς, ὅπερ νηστεύειν προσῆκεν, ἀλλ᾽ οὐχ ἑορ-
τάζειν· ἐν ὅσῳ γὰρ ὁ δημιουργὸς ὑπὸ γῆν τυγχάνει,
ἰσχυρότερον τὸ περὶ αὐτοῦ πένθος τῆς κατὰ τὴν
δημιουργίαν χαρᾶς, ὅτι ὁ δημιουργὸς τῶν ἑαυτοῦ
δημιουργημάτων φύσει τε καὶ ἀξίᾳ τιμιώτερος.

24. Ὅταν δὲ προσεύχησθε, μὴ γίνεσθε ὡς οἱ ὑποκριταί, [2]
ἀλλ᾽ ὡς ὁ Κύριος ἡμῖν ἐν τῷ εὐαγγελίῳ διετάξατο, οὕτω προσ-
εύχεσθε· Πάτερ ἡμῶν ὁ ἐν τοῖς οὐρανοῖς, ἁγιασθήτω τὸ ὄνομά
σου· ἐλθέτω ἡ βασιλεία σου· γενηθήτω τὸ θέλημά σου ὡς ἐν
οὐρανῷ καὶ ἐπὶ τῆς γῆς· τὸν ἄρτον ἡμῶν τὸν ἐπιούσιον δὸς
ἡμῖν σήμερον· καὶ ἄφες ἡμῖν τὰ ὀφειλήματα ἡμῶν, ὡς καὶ

E

ἡμεῖς ἀφίεμεν τοῖς ὀφειλέταις ἡμῶν· καὶ μὴ εἰσενέγκῃς ἡμᾶς
εἰς πειρασμόν, ἀλλὰ ῥῦσαι ἡμᾶς ἀπὸ τοῦ πονηροῦ· ὅτι σοῦ
ἐστιν ἡ βασιλεία καὶ ἡ δύναμις καὶ ἡ δόξα εἰς τοὺς αἰῶνας·
[3] ἀμήν. Τρὶς τῆς ἡμέρας οὕτω προσεύχεσθε, προπαρασ-
κευάζοντες ἑαυτοὺς ἀξίους τῆς υἱοθεσίας τοῦ Πατρός, ἵνα μή, ἀναξίως ὑμῶν αὐτὸν πατέρα καλούν-
των, ὀνειδισθῆτε ὑπ᾽ αὐτοῦ, ὡς καὶ ὁ Ἰσραὴλ ὅ
ποτε πρωτότοκος υἱὸς ἤκουσεν ὅτι· Εἰ πατήρ εἰμι
ἐγώ, ποῦ ἐστιν ἡ δόξα μου; καὶ εἰ κύριός εἰμι,
ποῦ ἐστιν ὁ φόβος μου; δόξα γὰρ πατέρων ὁσιό-
της παίδων, καὶ τιμὴ δεσποτῶν οἰκετῶν φόβος,
ὥσπερ οὖν τὸ ἐναντίον ἀδοξία καὶ ἀναρχία· Δι᾽
ὑμᾶς γὰρ βλασφημεῖται τὸ ὄνομά μου ἐν τοῖς
ἔθνεσι.

25. Γίνεσθε δὲ πάντοτε εὐχάριστοι, ὡς πιστοὶ
[IX. 1] καὶ εὐγνώμονες δοῦλοι, περὶ μὲν τῆς εὐχαριστίας οὕτω
[3] λέγοντες· "Εὐχαριστοῦμέν σοι, Πάτερ ἡμῶν, ὑπὲρ τῆς ζωῆς,
ἧς ἐγνώρισας ἡμῖν διὰ Ἰησοῦ τοῦ παιδός σου, δι᾽ οὗ καὶ τὰ
πάντα ἐποίησας καὶ τῶν ὅλων προνοεῖς, ὃν καὶ
ἀπέστειλας ἐπὶ σωτηρίᾳ τῇ ἡμετέρᾳ γενέσθαι ἄνθρωπον, ὃν καὶ συνεχώρησας παθεῖν καὶ ἀποθανεῖν,
ὃν καὶ ἀναστήσας εὐδόκησας δοξάσαι καὶ ἐκάθισας
ἐκ δεξιῶν σου, δι᾽ οὗ καὶ ἐπηγγείλω ἡμῖν τὴν ἀνάστασιν τῶν νεκρῶν. Σύ, δέσποτα παντοκράτορ, Θεὲ
[4] αἰώνιε, ὥσπερ ἦν τοῦτο διεσκορπισμένον καὶ συναχθὲν ἐγένετο
εἰς ἄρτος, οὕτω συνάγαγέ σου τὴν ἐκκλησίαν ἀπὸ τῶν περάτων τῆς γῆς εἰς τὴν σὴν βασιλείαν. Ἔτι εὐχαριστοῦμεν,
Πάτερ ἡμῶν, ὑπὲρ τοῦ τιμίου αἵματος Ἰησοῦ Χριστοῦ τοῦ ἐκχυθέντος ὑπὲρ ἡμῶν καὶ τοῦ τιμίου σώ-
ματος, οὗ καὶ ἀντίτυπα ταῦτα ἐπιτελοῦμεν, αὐτοῦ

διαταξαμένου ἡμῖν καταγγέλλειν τὸν αὐτοῦ θάνα-
τον· δι᾽ αὐτοῦ γάρ σοι καὶ ἡ δόξα εἰς τοὺς αἰῶνας· [4]
ἀμήν." Μηδεὶς δὲ ἐσθιέτω ἐξ αὐτῶν τῶν ἀμυήτων, ἀλλὰ [5]
μόνοι οἱ βεβαπτισμένοι εἰς τὸν τοῦ Κυρίου θάνατον.
Εἰ δέ τις ἀμύητος κρύψας ἑαυτὸν μεταλάβοι,
κρίμα αἰώνιον φάγεται, ὅτι μὴ ὢν τῆς εἰς Χριστὸν
πίστεως μετέλαβεν ὧν οὐ θέμις, εἰς τιμωρίαν ἑαυ-
τοῦ· εἰ δέ τις κατὰ ἄγνοιαν μεταλάβοι, τοῦτον
τάχιον στοιχειώσαντες μυήσατε, ὅπως μὴ κατα-
φρονητὴς ἐξέλθοι.

26. Μετὰ δὲ τὴν μετάληψιν οὕτως εὐχαριστήσατε. [X. 1]
"Εὐχαριστοῦμέν σοι, ὁ Θεὸς καὶ Πατὴρ Ἰησοῦ τοῦ σωτῆρος ἡμῶν, ὑπὲρ τοῦ ἁγίου ὀνόματός σου, οὗ κατεσκήνωσας ἐν ἡμῖν, καὶ ὑπὲρ τῆς γνώσεως καὶ πίστεως καὶ ἀγά-
πης καὶ ἀθανασίας, ἧς ἔδωκας ἡμῖν διὰ Ἰησοῦ τοῦ παιδός [3]
σου. Σύ, δέσποτα παντοκράτορ, ὁ Θεὸς τῶν ὅλων, ὁ κτίσας
τὸν κόσμον καὶ τὰ ἐν αὐτῷ δι᾽ αὐτοῦ, καὶ νόμον κατεφύ-
τευσας ταῖς ψυχαῖς ἡμῶν, καὶ τὰ πρὸς μετάληψιν
εὐτρεπίσας ἀνθρώποις· ὁ Θεὸς τῶν ἁγίων καὶ ἀμέμ-
πτων πατέρων ἡμῶν, Ἀβραὰμ καὶ Ἰσαὰκ καὶ
Ἰακώβ, τῶν πιστῶν δούλων σου· ὁ δυνατὸς Θεός,
ὁ πιστὸς καὶ ἀληθινὸς καὶ ἀψευδὴς ἐν ταῖς ἐπαγ-
γελίαις· ὁ ἀποστείλας ἐπὶ γῆς Ἰησοῦν τὸν Χρισ-
τόν σου ἀνθρώποις συναναστραφῆναι ὡς ἄνθρωπον, Θεὸν ὄντα Λόγον καὶ ἄνθρωπον, καὶ τὴν πλάνην
πρόρριζον ἀνελεῖν· αὐτὸς καὶ νῦν δι᾽ αὐτοῦ μνήσθητι [5]
τῆς ἁγίας σου ἐκκλησίας ταύτης, ἣν περιεποιήσω τῷ
τιμίῳ αἵματι τοῦ Χριστοῦ σου, καὶ ῥῦσαι αὐτὴν ἀπὸ παντὸς
πονηροῦ καὶ τελείωσον αὐτὴν ἐν τῇ ἀγάπῃ σου καὶ τῇ ἀλη-
θείᾳ σου, καὶ συνάγαγε πάντας ἡμᾶς εἰς τὴν σὴν βασιλείαν,

[6] ἦν ἡτοίμασας αὐτῇ. Μαραναθά· ὡσαννὰ τῷ υἱῷ Δαβίδ
εὐλογημένος ὁ ἐρχόμενος ἐν ὀνόματι Κυρίου, Θεὸς
[6] Κύριος ὁ ἐπιφανεὶς ἡμῖν ἐν σαρκί." Εἴ τις ἅγιος
[7] προσερχέσθω· εἰ δέ τις οὐκ ἔστι, γινέσθω διὰ μετανοίας,
Ἐπιτρέπετε δὲ καὶ τοῖς πρεσβυτέροις ὑμῶν εὐχαριστεῖν.

27. Περὶ δὲ τοῦ μύρου οὕτως εὐχαριστήσατε·
"Εὐχαριστοῦμέν σοι, Θεὲ δημιουργὲ τῶν ὅλων,
καὶ ὑπὲρ τῆς εὐωδίας τοῦ μύρου, καὶ ὑπὲρ τοῦ ἀθα-
νάτου αἰῶνος, οὗ ἐγνώρισας ἡμῖν διὰ Ἰησοῦ τοῦ
παιδός σου· ὅτι σοῦ ἐστιν ἡ δόξα καὶ ἡ δύναμις
εἰς τοὺς αἰῶνας· ἀμήν."

[XI. 1] Ὃς ἐὰν ἐλθὼν οὕτως εὐχαριστῇ, προσδέξασθε αὐτὸν ὡς
[2] Χριστοῦ μαθητήν· ἐὰν δὲ ἄλλην διδαχὴν κηρύσσῃ παρ'
ἣν ὑμῖν παρέδωκεν ὁ Χριστὸς δι' ἡμῶν, τῷ τοιούτῳ
μὴ συγχωρεῖτε εὐχαριστεῖν· ὑβρίζει γὰρ ὁ τοιοῦτος
τὸν Θεὸν ἤπερ δοξάζει.

[XII. 1] 28. Πᾶς δὲ ὁ ἐρχόμενος πρὸς ὑμᾶς, δοκιμασθείς, οὕτω
δεχέσθω· σύνεσιν γὰρ ἔχετε, καὶ δύνασθε γνῶναι δεξιὰν ἢ
ἀριστερὰν καὶ διακρῖναι ψευδοδιδασκάλους διδασκάλων. Ἐλθόντι μέντοι τῷ διδασκάλῳ ἐκ ψυχῆς
ἐπιχορηγήσατε τὰ δέοντα· τῷ δὲ ψευδοδιδασκάλῳ,
δώσετε μὲν τὰ δέοντα πρὸς τὴν χρείαν, οὐ παρα-
δέξεσθε δὲ αὐτοῦ τὴν πλάνην, οὔτε μὴν συμπρο-
[XIII.1,2] σεύξεσθε αὐτῷ, ἵνα μὴ συμμιανθῆτε αὐτῷ. Πᾶς
προφήτης ἀληθινὸς ἢ διδάσκαλος ἐρχόμενος πρὸς ὑμᾶς
ἄξιός ἐστι τῆς τροφῆς ὡς ἐργάτης λόγου δικαιοσύνης.
[3] 29. Πᾶσαν ἀπαρχὴν γεννημάτων ληνοῦ, ἅλωνος, βοῶν τε
καὶ προβάτων δώσεις τοῖς ἱερεῦσιν, ἵνα εὐλογηθῶσιν
αἱ ἀποθῆκαι τῶν ταμιείων σου καὶ τὰ ἐκφόρια τῆς

γῆς σου, καὶ στηριχθῇς σίτῳ καὶ οἴνῳ καὶ ἐλαίῳ,
καὶ αὐξηθῇ τὰ βουκόλια τῶν βοῶν σου καὶ τὰ
ποίμνια τῶν προβάτων σου· πᾶσαν δεκάτην δώσεις τῷ ὀρφανῷ καὶ τῇ χήρᾳ, τῷ πτωχῷ καὶ τῷ
προσηλύτῳ. Πᾶσαν ἀπαρχὴν ἄρτων, θερμῶν, κερά- [5, 6]
μιον οἴνου ἢ ἐλαίου ἢ μέλιτος ἢ ἀκροδρύων, σταφυλῆς
ἢ τῶν ἄλλων τὴν ἀπαρχὴν δώσεις τοῖς ἱερεῦσιν· ἀργυρίου δὲ καὶ ἱματισμοῦ καὶ παντὸς κτήματος τῷ ὀρφανῷ [7]
καὶ τῇ χήρᾳ.

30. Τὴν ἀναστάσιμον τοῦ Κυρίου ἡμέραν, τὴν κυριακήν [XIV. 1]
φαμεν, συνέρχεσθε ἀδιαλείπτως, εὐχαριστοῦντες τῷ Θεῷ
καὶ ἐξομολογούμενοι ἐφ᾽ οἷς εὐηργέτησεν ἡμᾶς ὁ Θεὸς
διὰ Χριστοῦ ῥυσάμενος ἀγνοίας, πλάνης, δεσμῶν·
ὅπως ἄμεμπτος ἡ θυσία ὑμῶν ᾖ καὶ εὐανάφορος Θεῷ, [1]
τῷ εἰπόντι περὶ τῆς οἰκουμενικῆς αὐτοῦ ἐκκλησίας
ὅτι· Ἐν παντὶ τόπῳ προσενεχθήσεταί μοι θυμίαμα καὶ [3]
θυσία καθαρά· ὅτι βασιλεὺς μέγας ἐγώ εἰμι, λέγει Κύριος
παντοκράτωρ, καὶ τὸ ὄνομά μου θαυμαστὸν ἐν τοῖς ἔθνεσιν.

31. Προχειρίσασθε δὲ ἐπισκόπους ἀξίους τοῦ Κυρίου [XV. 1]
καὶ πρεσβυτέρους, καὶ διακόνους, ἄνδρας εὐλαβεῖς, δικαίους, πραεῖς, ἀφιλαργύρους, φιλαλήθεις, δεδοκιμασμένους,
ὁσίους, ἀπροσωπολήπτους, δυναμένους διδάσκειν
τὸν λόγον τῆς εὐσεβείας, ὀρθοτομοῦντας ἐν τοῖς
τοῦ Κυρίου δόγμασιν. Ὑμεῖς δὲ τιμᾶτε τούτους ὡς [2]
πατέρας, ὡς κυρίους, ὡς εὐεργέτας, ὡς τοῦ εὖ εἶναι
αἰτίους.

Ἐλέγχετε δὲ ἀλλήλους μὴ ἐν ὀργῇ, ἀλλ᾽ ἐν μακροθυμίᾳ [3]
μετὰ χρηστότητος καὶ εἰρήνης· Πάντα τὰ προστε-
ταγμένα ὑμῖν ὑπὸ τοῦ Κυρίου φυλάξατε. Γρηγο- [XVI. 1]
ρεῖτε ὑπὲρ τῆς ζωῆς ὑμῶν. Ἔστωσαν αἱ ὀσφύες ὑμῶν περιε-

ζωσμέναι καὶ οἱ λύχνοι καιόμενοι, καὶ ὑμεῖς ὅμοιοι ἀνθρώποις προσδεχομένοις τὸν κύριον ἑαυτῶν πότε
ἥξει, ἑσπέρας ἢ πρωὶ ἢ ἀλεκτοροφωνίας ἢ μεσο-
νυκτίου ᾗ γὰρ ὥρᾳ οὐ προσδοκῶσιν, ἐλεύσεται ὁ
Κύριος, καὶ ἐὰν αὐτῷ ἀνοίξωσι, μακάριοι οἱ δοῦλοι
ἐκεῖνοι, ὅτι εὑρέθησαν γρηγοροῦντες· ὅτι περιζώ-
σεται καὶ ἀνακλινεῖ αὐτοὺς καὶ παρελθὼν διακο-
νήσει αὐτοῖς. Νήφετε οὖν καὶ προσεύχεσθε μὴ
[2] ὑπνῶσαι εἰς θάνατον· οὐ γὰρ ὀνήσει ὑμᾶς τὰ πρότερα
κατορθώματα, ἐὰν εἰς τὰ ἔσχατα ὑμῶν ἀποπλανηθῆτε τῆς
πίστεως τῆς ἀληθοῦς.

[3]   32. Ἐν γὰρ ταῖς ἐσχάταις ἡμέραις πληθυνθήσονται οἱ
ψευδοπροφῆται καὶ οἱ φθορεῖς τοῦ λόγου, καὶ στραφήσον-
ται τὰ πρόβατα εἰς λύκους καὶ ἡ ἀγάπη εἰς μῖσος· πληθυν-
θείσης γὰρ τῆς ἀνομίας ψυγήσεται ἡ ἀγάπη τῶν πολ-
[4] λῶν· μισήσουσι γὰρ ἀλλήλους οἱ ἄνθρωποι καὶ διώξουσι
καὶ προδώσουσι. Καὶ τότε φανήσεται ὁ κοσμοπλάνος, ὁ τῆς
ἀληθείας ἐχθρός, ὁ τοῦ ψεύδους προστάτης, ὃν ὁ
Κύριος Ἰησοῦς ἀνελεῖ τῷ πνεύματι τοῦ στόματος
[5] αὐτοῦ, ὁ διὰ χειλέων ἀναιρῶν ἀσεβῆ· καὶ πολλοὶ
σκανδαλισθήσονται ἐπ' αὐτῷ, οἱ δὲ ὑπομείναντες εἰς τέλος,
[6] οὗτοι σωθήσονται. Καὶ τότε φανήσεται τὸ σημεῖον τοῦ
υἱοῦ τοῦ ἀνθρώπου ἐν τῷ οὐρανῷ, εἶτα φωνὴ σάλπιγγος
ἔσται δι' ἀρχαγγέλου καὶ μεταξὺ ἀναβίωσις τῶν κεκοιμη-
[7] μένων· καὶ τότε ἥξει ὁ Κύριος καὶ πάντες οἱ ἅγιοι μετ' αὐτοῦ
[8] ἐν συσσεισμῷ ἐπάνω τῶν νεφελῶν μετ' ἀγγέλων δυνάμεως αὐτοῦ ἐπὶ θρόνου βασιλείας κατακρῖναι τὸν
κοσμοπλάνον διάβολον, καὶ ἀποδοῦναι ἑκάστῳ
κατὰ τὴν πρᾶξιν αὐτοῦ. Τότε ἀπελεύσονται οἱ
μὲν πονηροὶ εἰς αἰώνιον κόλασιν, οἱ δὲ δίκαιοι

πορεύσονται εἰς ζωὴν αἰώνιον, κληρονομοῦντες ἐκεῖνα ἃ ὀφθαλμὸς οὐκ εἶδεν καὶ οὖς οὐκ ἤκουσεν καὶ ἐπὶ καρδίαν ἀνθρώπου οὐκ ἀνέβη, ἃ ἡτοίμασεν ὁ Θεὸς τοῖς ἀγαπῶσιν αὐτόν· καὶ χαρήσονται ἐν τῇ βασιλείᾳ τοῦ Θεοῦ τῇ ἐν Χριστῷ Ἰησοῦ.

A SUMMARY OF THE PRINCIPAL PARALLEL PASSAGES ADDUCED IN ILLUSTRATION

OF THE Διδαχή[a].

Διδαχή. Chap.	Scripture.	Other Writings.	Const. Ap. Book VII.[b] Chap.
I. 1.		Barn. xviii. 1 (Comp. xix. 2; xx. 1).	1.
,, 2.	Matt. xxii. 37. ,, vii. 12.	Barn. xix. 1, 2, 5ᶜ.	2.
,, 3.	,, v. 44, 46. Luke vi. 27, 28.		,,
,, 4.	Matt. v. 39—41 (43). Luke vi. 29, 30.	The first clause peculiar to Δ.	,,
,, 5.	Matt. v. 25, 26. Luke vi. 30.	Herm. Mand. ii. 4—6 (not close).	,,
,, 6.		Unknown.	
II. 1.	Matt. xxii. 39.		,,
,, 2.		Barn. xix. 4ᵃ, 5ᵈ, 6ᵃ. Δ. fuller, and the order different.	2, 3.
,, 3.		Barn. xix. 4ᶜ. Δ. fuller.	3, 4.
,, 4.		Barn. xix. 7ᵃ.	4.
,, 5.			,,
,, 6.		Barn. xix. 6ᵇ, 3ᵈ. Δ. fuller.	4, 5.
,, 7.		Barn. xix. 11ᵈ, 5ᶜ, not very close.	5.
III. 1—6.			5, 6.
,, 7.	Matt. v. 5.	Barn. xix. 4ᵈ.	7.
,, 8.		,, ,, 4ᵈ. Δ. fuller.	8.
,, 9.		,, ,, 3ᵃ, 3ᶜ, 6ᶜ.	,,
,, 10.		,, ,, 6ᵈ.	,,
IV. 1.		,, ,, 9ᵇ, 10ᵃ, with considerable differences.	9.

[a] The small letters, a, b, c, d, denote respectively the first or other parts of the sections.   [b] See also Illustrations, Nos. IV. and V.

Διδαχή. CHAP.		Scripture.	Other Writings.	Const. Ap. Book VII. CHAP.
IV.	2.		Barn. xix. 10^b. Δ. fuller.	9.
„	8.		Barn. xix. 12^a, 11^c, 4^c.	10.
„	4.		„ „ 5^a.	11.
„	5.		„ „ 9^a.	„
„	6.		„ „ 10^d.	12.
„	7.		„ „ 11^a, 11^b.	„
„	8.		„ „ 8^a. Δ.fuller.	„
„	9.		„ „ 5^c.	„
„	10.		„ „ 7^c, 7^d, 7^e.	13.
„	11.		„ „ 7^b.	„
„	12.		„ „ 2^g, 2^b.	14.
„	13.		„ „ 2^b, 11.	„
„	14.		„ 12^{b-d}. Δ. fuller.	17.
V.			Barn. xx., not close. Herm. Mand. viii. 3–5.	18.
VI.	1.		Barn. xviii. 1; xxi. 6^a.	19.
„	2.		„ xix. 8^c.	„
„	3.			20, 21.
VII.		Matt. xxviii. 19, not close.		22.
VIII.	1.	Matt. vi. 16, not close.		23.
„	2, 3.	Matt. vi. 5, 9—13.		24.
IX., X.		Luke xxii. 14, not close, much of the wording apparently influenced by St. John's phraseology.		25, 26.
IX.	4.	Matt. xxiv. 81.		25.
„	5.	„ vii. 6.		„
X.	5.	„ xxiv. 81.		26.
„	5.	„ xxv. 34.		„
„	6.	„ xxi. 9, 15.	Barn. xii. 10, 11 (1 Cor. xvi. 22).	„

Διδαχή. CHAP.	Scripture.	Other Writings.	Const. Ap. Book VII. CHAP.
XI. 1, 2.			
3—12.	Matt. x. 5. „ vii. 15. Luke ix. 1. „ x. 4, not closely.		27.
„ 7.	Matt. xii. 31.		„
„ 10.	„ xxiii. 3.		„
XII.	Compare Matt. x. 40—42.		28.
„ 3.	2 Thess. iii. 10.		„
XIII. 1, 2.	Matt. x. 10.		29.
„ 3,6,7.	1 Cor. ix. 13, 14. The special rule as to first-fruits based on Mosaic Law.		
XIV.	Matt. v. 23, 24. Mal. i. 11, 14.		30.
XV. 1, 2.			31.
„ 3.	Matt. v. 22. „ xviii. 15–17, 21.		„
XVI. 1.	Matt. xxiv. 42, 44. Luke xii. 35.		„
„ 2.		Barn. iv. 9.	
„ 3–8.	Matt. xxiv. 11, 10, 12, 10, 3, 30, 31.	Δ. fuller.	32.
„ 7.	Zech. xiv. 5.		„

ΔΙΔΑΧΗ

ΤΩΝ

ΔΩΔΕΚΑ ΑΠΟΣΤΟΛΩΝ.

ΔΙΔΑΧΗ

ΤΩΝ

ΔΩΔΕΚΑ ΑΠΟΣΤΟΛΩΝ.

Διδαχὴ Κυρίου διὰ τῶν δώδεκα ἀποστόλων τοῖς ἔθνεσιν.

[Κεφ. α΄.]

1. Ὁδοὶ δύο εἰσί, μία τῆς ζωῆς καὶ μία τοῦ θανάτου, διαφορὰ δὲ πολλὴ μεταξὺ τῶν δύο ὁδῶν.

2. Ἡ μὲν οὖν ὁδὸς τῆς ζωῆς ἐστιν αὕτη· πρῶτον, ἀγαπήσεις τὸν Θεὸν τὸν ποιήσαντά σε· δεύτερον, τὸν πλησίον σου ὡς σεαυτόν· πάντα δὲ ὅσα ἐὰν θελήσῃς μὴ γίνεσθαί σοι, καὶ σὺ ἄλλῳ μὴ ποίει.

3. Τούτων δὲ τῶν λόγων ἡ διδαχή ἐστιν αὕτη· Εὐλογεῖτε τοὺς καταρωμένους ὑμῖν καὶ προσεύχεσθε ὑπὲρ τῶν ἐχθρῶν ὑμῶν, νηστεύετε δὲ ὑπὲρ τῶν διωκόντων ὑμᾶς· ποία γὰρ χάρις, ἐὰν ἀγαπᾶτε τοὺς ἀγαπῶντας ὑμᾶς; οὐχὶ καὶ τὰ ἔθνη τὸ αὐτὸ ποιοῦσιν; ὑμεῖς δὲ ἀγαπᾶτε τοὺς μισοῦντας ὑμᾶς καὶ οὐχ ἕξετε ἐχθρόν.

4. Ἀπέχου τῶν σαρκικῶν καὶ σωματικῶν [a] ἐπιθυμιῶν. Ἐάν τίς σοι δῷ ῥάπισμα εἰς τὴν δεξιὰν σιαγόνα, στρέψον αὐτῷ καὶ τὴν ἄλλην, καὶ ἔσῃ τέλειος· ἐὰν ἀγγαρεύσῃ σέ τις μίλιον ἕν, ὕπαγε

[a] [κοσμικῶν, B.]

TEACHING

OF THE

TWELVE APOSTLES.

The Teaching of the Lord by the Twelve
Apostles to the Gentiles.

[Chap. I.]

1. There are two ways, one of life and one of death [a],
but a great difference between the two ways.

2. Now the way of life is this: first, Thou shalt
love God who made thee; secondly, thy neighbour as
thyself [b], and all things whatsoever thou wouldest not
should be done to thee, do thou also not do to another.

3. Now the teaching of these two sayings is this,
Bless them that curse you, and pray for your enemies [c],
but fast for them that persecute you; For what thank
is there if ye love them that love you? do not even
the Gentiles the same? But love ye them that hate
you, and ye shall not have an enemy.

4. Abstain from fleshly [d] and bodily lusts. If any
one give thee a blow on the right cheek [e] turn to him
the other also, and thou shalt be perfect. If any one
compel thee to go with him one mile, go with him

[a] Jer. xxi. 8.   [b] Matt. xxii. 37, 39.   [c] Luke vi. 28.
[d] 1 Pet. ii. 11.   [e] Matt. v. 39.

μετ᾽ αὐτοῦ δύο· ἐὰν ἄρῃ τις τὸ ἱμάτιόν σου, δὸς αὐτῷ καὶ τὸν χιτῶνα· ἐὰν λάβῃ τις ἀπὸ σοῦ τὸ σόν, μὴ ἀπαίτει· οὐδὲ γὰρ δύνασαι.

5. Παντὶ τῷ αἰτοῦντί σε δίδου καὶ μὴ ἀπαίτει· πᾶσι γὰρ θέλει δίδοσθαι ὁ πατὴρ ἐκ τῶν ἰδίων χαρισμάτων. Μακάριος ὁ διδοὺς κατὰ τὴν ἐντολήν· ἀθῶος γάρ ἐστιν· οὐαὶ τῷ λαμβάνοντι· εἰ μὲν γὰρ χρείαν ἔχων λαμβάνει τις, ἀθῶος ἔσται· ὁ δὲ μὴ χρείαν ἔχων δώσει δίκην, ἱνατί ἔλαβε καὶ εἰς τί, ἐν συνοχῇ δὲ γενόμενος ἐξετασθήσεται περὶ ὧν ἔπραξε, καὶ οὐκ ἐξελεύσεται ἐκεῖθεν μέχρι οὗ ἀποδῷ τὸν ἔσχατον κοδράντην.

6. Ἀλλὰ καὶ περὶ τούτου δὲ[b] εἴρηται· ἱδρωτάτω[c] ἡ ἐλεημοσύνη σου εἰς τὰς χεῖράς σου, μέχρι[d] ἂν γνῷς τίνι δῷς.

[Κεφ. β᾽.]

1. Δευτέρα δὲ ἐντολὴ τῆς διδαχῆς.

2. Οὐ φονεύσεις, οὐ μοιχεύσεις, οὐ παιδοφθορήσεις, οὐ πορνεύσεις, οὐ κλέψεις, οὐ μαγεύσεις, οὐ φαρμακεύσεις, οὐ φονεύσεις τέκνον ἐν φθορᾷ, οὐδὲ γεννηθέντα[e] ἀποκτενεῖς. Οὐκ ἐπιθυμήσεις τὰ τοῦ πλησίον,

3. Οὐκ ἐπιορκήσεις, οὐ ψευδομαρτυρήσεις, οὐ κακολογήσεις, οὐ μνησικακήσεις.

4. Οὐκ ἔσῃ διγνώμων οὐδὲ δίγλωσσος· παγὶς γὰρ θανάτου ἡ διγλωσσία.

[b] [δὴ, B., &c.] [c] [ἱδρωσάτω, B. Hr.; ἱδρυσάτω, Hl.]
[d] [μέχρις, B., &c.] [e] [γεννηθὲν, B., &c.]

twain; if any one take away thy cloak, give him thy coat also; If any one take from thee what is thine ask it not back', for neither canst thou.

5. Give to every one that asketh of thee, and ask not back, for the Father wills that from our own blessings we should give to all. Blessed is he that giveth according to the commandment, for he is guiltless. Woe to him that taketh; for if indeed any one having need taketh he shall be guiltless, but he that hath not need shall give account, wherefore he took anything and for what purpose, and being in distress shall be examined concerning the things that he did, and he shall not come out thence till he have paid the last farthing'.

6. But concerning this also it hath been said, Let thine alms sweat into thine hands till thou know to whom thou givest.

[CHAP. II.]

1. And the second commandment of the teaching is:

2. Thou shalt not kill, thou shalt not commit adultery, thou shalt not corrupt boys, thou shalt not commit fornication, thou shalt not steal, thou shalt not use witchcraft, thou shalt not use enchantments, thou shalt not procure abortion, nor shalt thou kill the new-born child, thou shalt not covet thy neighbour's goods.

3. Thou shalt not forswear thyself, thou shalt not bear false witness, thou shalt not revile, thou shalt not bear malice.

4. Thou shalt not be double-minded nor double-tongued; for duplicity of tongue is a snare of death.

' Luke vi. 30.   ' Matt. v. 26.

5. Οὐκ ἔσται ὁ λόγος σου ψευδής, οὐ κενός, ἀλλὰ μεμεστωμένος πράξει.

6. Οὐκ ἔσῃ πλεονέκτης οὐδὲ ἅρπαξ οὐδὲ ὑποκριτὴς οὐδὲ κακοήθης οὐδὲ ὑπερήφανος. Οὐ λήψῃ βουλὴν πονηρὰν κατὰ τοῦ πλησίον σου.

7. Οὐ μισήσεις πάντα ἄνθρωπον, ἀλλὰ οὓς μὲν ἐλέγξεις, περὶ δὲ ὧν προσεύξῃ, οὓς δὲ ἀγαπήσεις ὑπὲρ τὴν ψυχήν σου.

[Κεφ. γ΄.]

1. Τέκνον μου, φεῦγε ἀπὸ παντὸς πονηροῦ καὶ ἀπὸ παντὸς ὁμοίου αὐτοῦ.

2. Μὴ γίνου ὀργίλος· [f] ὁδηγεῖ γὰρ ἡ ὀργὴ πρὸς τὸν φόνον· μηδὲ ζηλωτὴς μηδὲ ἐριστικὸς μηδὲ θυμικός· ἐκ γὰρ τούτων ἁπάντων φόνοι γεννῶνται.

3. Τέκνον μου, μὴ γίνου ἐπιθυμητής· ὁδηγεῖ γὰρ ἡ ἐπιθυμία πρὸς τὴν πορνείαν· μηδὲ αἰσχρολόγος μηδὲ ὑψηλόφθαλμος· ἐκ γὰρ τούτων ἁπάντων μοιχεῖαι γεννῶνται.

4. Τέκνον μου, μὴ γίνου οἰωνοσκόπος· ἐπειδὴ ὁδηγεῖ εἰς τὴν εἰδωλολατρίαν [g] μηδὲ ἐπαοιδὸς μηδὲ μαθηματικὸς μηδὲ περικαθαίρων, μηδὲ θέλε αὐτὰ βλέπειν· ἐκ γὰρ τούτων ἁπάντων εἰδωλολατρία [h] γεννᾶται.

5. Τέκνον μου, μὴ γίνου ψεύστης· ἐπειδὴ ὁδηγεῖ τὸ ψεῦσμα εἰς τὴν κλοπήν· μηδὲ φιλάργυρος μηδὲ κενόδοξος· ἐκ γὰρ τούτων ἁπάντων κλοπαὶ γεννῶνται.

---

[f] [ὀργίλος, B.]   [g] [εἰδωλολατρείαν, B. Hl.]

[h] [εἰδωλολατρεία, B. Hl.]

5. Thy speech shall not be false nor vain, but filled by deed.

6. Thou shalt not be covetous, nor an extortioner, nor a hypocrite, nor malignant, nor haughty. Thou shalt not take evil counsel against thy neighbour.

7. Thou shalt hate no man, but some thou shalt rebuke, and for some thou shalt pray, and some thou shalt love above thine own soul.

[CHAP. III.]

1. My child, flee from all evil, and from all that is like unto it [h].

2. Be not soon angry, for anger leadeth to murder, nor given to party spirit, nor contentious, nor quick-tempered, for from all these are generated murders.

3. My child, be not lustful, for lust leadeth to fornication, neither be a filthy talker, nor a lifter up of the eyes [to sin], for from all these are generated adulteries.

4. My child, be not thou an observer of birds [for divination], for it leadeth to idolatry, nor a charmer, nor an astrologer, nor a user of purifications, nor be thou willing to look on those things, for from all these is generated idolatry.

5. My child, be not a liar, for lying leadeth to theft, nor a lover of money, nor fond of vainglory, for from all these things are generated thefts.

[h] 1 Thess. v. 22.

F

6. Τέκνον μου, μὴ γίνου γόγγυσος· ἐπειδὴ ὁδηγεῖ εἰς τὴν βλασφημίαν· μηδὲ αὐθάδης μηδὲ πονηρόφρων· ἐκ γὰρ τούτων ἁπάντων βλασφημίαι γεννῶνται.

7. Ἴσθι δὲ πραΰς, ἐπεὶ οἱ πραεῖς κληρονομήσουσι τὴν γῆν.

8. Γίνου μακρόθυμος καὶ ἐλεήμων καὶ ἄκακος καὶ ἡσύχιος καὶ ἀγαθὸς καὶ τρέμων τοὺς λόγους διὰ παντός, οὓς ἤκουσας.

9. Οὐχ ὑψώσεις σεαυτὸν οὐδὲ δώσεις τῇ ψυχῇ σου θράσος. Οὐ κολληθήσεται ἡ ψυχή σου μετὰ ὑψηλῶν, ἀλλὰ μετὰ δικαίων καὶ ταπεινῶν ἀναστραφήσῃ.

10. Τὰ συμβαίνοντά σοι ἐνεργήματα ὡς ἀγαθὰ προσδέξῃ, εἰδὼς ὅτι ἄτερ Θεοῦ οὐδὲν γίνεται.

[Κεφ. δ΄.]

1. Τέκνον μου, τοῦ λαλοῦντός σοι τὸν λόγον τοῦ Θεοῦ μνησθήσῃ νυκτὸς καὶ ἡμέρας, τιμήσεις δὲ αὐτὸν ὡς Κύριον· ὅθεν γὰρ ἡ κυριότης λαλεῖται, ἐκεῖ Κύριός ἐστιν.

2. Ἐκζητήσεις δὲ καθ᾽ ἡμέραν τὰ πρόσωπα τῶν ἁγίων, ἵνα ἐπαναπαῆς[1] τοῖς λόγοις αὐτῶν.

3. Οὐ ποθήσεις[k] σχίσμα, εἰρηνεύσεις δὲ μαχομένους· κρινεῖς δικαίως, οὐ λήψῃ πρόσωπον ἐλέγξαι ἐπὶ παραπτώμασιν.

---

[1] [ἐπαναπαύῃ, B.; ἐπαναπαῇς, Hr. Hl.]
[k] [ποιήσεις, Hr. Hl.]

6. My child, be not a murmurer, for it leadeth to blasphemy, neither self-willed, nor evil-minded, for from all these are generated blasphemies.

7. But be thou meek, for the meek shall inherit the earth [1].

8. Be thou long-suffering, and merciful, and harmless, and quiet, and good, and trembling continually at the words which thou hast heard [k].

9. Thou shalt not exalt thyself, nor shalt thou give presumption to thy soul. Thy soul shalt not be joined to the lofty, but with the just and lowly shalt thou converse.

10. The events that happen to thee shalt thou accept as good, knowing that without God nothing taketh place.

[CHAP. IV.]

1. My child, thou shalt remember night and day him that speaketh to thee the word of God, and thou shalt honour him as the Lord, for whence the Lordship is spoken of, there is the Lord.

2. But thou shalt seek out day by day the faces of the saints, that thou mayest rest in their words.

3. Thou shalt not desire division, but shalt make peace between those at strife, thou shalt judge justly. Thou shalt not respect a person in rebuking for transgressions.

---

[1] Matt. v. 5.   [k] Isa. lxvi. 2, 5.

4. Οὐ διψυχήσεις, πότερον ἔσται ἢ οὔ.

5. Μὴ γίνου πρὸς μὲν τὸ λαβεῖν ἐκτείνων τὰς χεῖρας, πρὸς δὲ τὸ δοῦναι συσπῶν.

6. Ἐὰν ἔχῃς, διὰ τῶν χειρῶν σου δώσεις λύτρωσιν ἁμαρτιῶν σου.

7. Οὐ διστάσεις δοῦναι οὐδὲ διδοὺς γογγύσεις· γνώσῃ γὰρ τίς ἐστιν ἡ[1] τοῦ μισθοῦ καλὸς ἀνταποδότης.

8. Οὐκ ἀποστραφήσῃ τὸν ἐνδεόμενον, συγκοινωνήσεις δὲ πάντα τῷ ἀδελφῷ σου καὶ οὐκ ἐρεῖς ἴδια εἶναι· εἰ γὰρ ἐν τῷ ἀθανάτῳ κοινωνοί ἐστε, πόσῳ μᾶλλον ἐν τοῖς θνητοῖς;

9. Οὐκ ἀρεῖς τὴν χεῖρά σου ἀπὸ τοῦ υἱοῦ σου ἢ ἀπὸ τῆς θυγατρός σου, ἀλλὰ ἀπὸ νεότητος διδάξεις τὸν φόβον τοῦ Θεοῦ.

10. Οὐκ ἐπιτάξεις δούλῳ σου ἢ παιδίσκῃ, τοῖς ἐπὶ τὸν αὐτὸν Θεὸν ἐλπίζουσι[m], ἐν πικρίᾳ σου, μήποτε οὐ μὴ φοβηθήσονται τὸν ἐπ' ἀμφοτέροις Θεόν· οὐ γὰρ ἔρχεται κατὰ πρόσωπον καλέσαι, ἀλλ' ἐφ' οὓς τὸ πνεῦμα ἡτοίμασεν.

11. Ὑμεῖς δὲ δοῦλοι[n] ὑποταγήσεσθε τοῖς κυρίοις ἡμῶν[o] ὡς τύπῳ Θεοῦ ἐν αἰσχύνῃ καὶ φόβῳ.

12. Μισήσεις πᾶσαν ὑπόκρισιν καὶ πᾶν ὃ μὴ ἀρεστὸν τῷ Κυρίῳ.

13. Οὐ μὴ ἐγκαταλίπῃς ἐντολὰς Κυρίου, φυλάξεις δὲ ἃ παρέλαβες, μήτε προστιθεὶς μήτε ἀφαιρῶν.

---

[1] [ὁ, B., &c.]
[a] [οἱ δοῦλοι, B. Hr. Hl.]

[m] [ἐλπίζουσιν, B., &c.]
[o] [ὑμῶν, B., &c.]

4. Thou shalt not be of two minds whether it shall be or not.

5. Be not one that stretcheth out his hands to receive, but shutteth them close for giving [m].

6. If thou hast, thou shalt give with thine hands a ransom for thy sins [n].

7. Thou shalt not hesitate to give, nor when thou givest shalt thou murmur, for thou shalt know who is the good recompenser of the reward.

8. Thou shalt not turn away from him that needeth, but shalt share all things with thy brother, and shalt not say that they are thine own, for if ye are fellow-sharers in that which is imperishable, how much more in perishable things?

9. Thou shalt not take away thine hand from thy son or from thy daughter, but from their youth up shalt thou teach them the fear of God.

10. Thou shalt not in thy bitterness lay commands on thy man-servant, or thy maid-servant, who hope in the same God, lest they should not fear Him who is God over [you] both, for He cometh not to call [men] according to the outward appearance, but to those whom the Spirit hath prepared.

11. But ye, servants, shall be subject to your masters as to a figure of God in reverence and fear.

12. Thou shalt hate all hypocrisy, and everything which is not pleasing to the Lord.

13. Thou shalt not forsake the commandments of the Lord, but shalt keep what thou hast received, neither adding [thereto] nor taking away [from it] [o].

[m] Ecclus. iv. 31.   [n] Cf. Dan. iv. 27; Job iv. 10.
[o] Deut. xii. 32.

14. Ἐν ἐκκλησίᾳ ἐξομολογήσῃ τὰ παραπτώματά σου, καὶ οὐ προσελεύσῃ ἐπὶ προσευχήν σου ἐν συνειδήσει πονηρᾷ. Αὕτη ἐστὶν ἡ ὁδὸς τῆς ζωῆς.

[Κεφ. ε´.]

1. Ἡ δὲ τοῦ θανάτου ὁδός ἐστιν αὕτη· πρῶτον πάντων πονηρά ἐστι καὶ κατάρας μεστή· φόνοι, μοιχεῖαι, ἐπιθυμίαι, πορνεῖαι, κλοπαί, εἰδωλολατρίαι[p], μαγεῖαι, φαρμακίαι[q], ἁρπαγαί, ψευδομαρτυρίαι, ὑποκρίσεις, διπλοκαρδία, δόλος, ὑπερηφανία, κακία, αὐθάδεια, πλεονεξία, αἰσχρολογία, ζηλοτυπία, θρασύτης, ὕψος, ἀλαζονεία. 2. Διῶκται ἀγαθῶν, μισοῦντες ἀλήθειαν, ἀγαπῶντες ψεῦδος, οὐ γινώσκοντες μισθὸν δικαιοσύνης, οὐ κολλώμενοι ἀγαθῷ οὐδὲ κρίσει δικαίᾳ, ἀγρυπνοῦντες οὐκ εἰς τὸ ἀγαθόν, ἀλλ᾽ εἰς τὸ πονηρόν. ὧν μακρὰν πραΰτης καὶ ὑπομονή, μάταια ἀγαπῶντες, διώκοντες ἀνταπόδομα, οὐκ ἐλεοῦντες πτωχόν, οὐ πονοῦντες ἐπὶ καταπονουμένῳ, οὐ γινώσκοντες τὸν ποιήσαντα αὐτούς, φονεῖς τέκνων, φθορεῖς πλάσματος Θεοῦ, ἀποστρεφόμενοι τὸν ἐνδεόμενον, καταπονοῦντες τὸν θλιβόμενον, πλουσίων παράκλητοι, πενήτων ἄνομοι κριταί, πανθαμάρτητοι· ῥυσθείητε, τέκνα, ἀπὸ τούτων ἁπάντων.

[p] [εἰδωλολατρεῖαι, B. H.]　　　[q] [φαρμακεῖαι, B. H.]

14. In the congregation thou shalt confess thy transgressions and shalt not come to thy prayer with an evil conscience. This is the way of life.

[CHAP. V.]

1. But the way of death is this. First of all it is evil and full of curse; murders, adulteries, lusts, fornications, thefts, idolatries, witchcrafts, sorceries, robberies, false-witnessings, hypocrisies, double-heartedness, deceit, pride, wickedness, self-will, covetousness, filthy-talking, jealousy, presumption, haughtiness, flattery.

2. Persecutors of the good, hating truth, loving a lie, not knowing the reward of righteousness, not cleaving to that which is good nor to righteous judgment, watchful not for the good but for the evil, far from whom is meekness and patience, loving vain things, seeking after reward, not pitying the poor, not toiling with him who is vexed with toil, not knowing Him that made them, murderers of children, destroyers of the image of God, turning away from him that is in need, vexing him that is afflicted, advocates of the rich, lawless judges of the poor, wholly sinful. May ye, children, be delivered from all these.

[Κεφ. ϛ'].

1. Ὅρα μή τις σε πλανήσῃ ἀπὸ ταύτης τῆς ὁδοῦ τῆς διδαχῆς, ἐπεὶ ʳ παρεκτὸς Θεοῦ σε διδάσκει.

2. Εἰ μὲν γὰρ δύνασαι βαστάσαι ὅλον τὸν ζυγὸν τοῦ Κυρίου, τέλειος ἔσῃ· εἰ δ' οὐ δύνασαι, ὃ δύνῃ τοῦτο ποίει.

3. Περὶ δὲ τῆς βρώσεως, ὃ δύνασαι βάστασον· ἀπὸ δὲ τοῦ εἰδωλοθύτου λίαν πρόσεχε· λατρεία γάρ ἐστι θεῶν νεκρῶν.

[Κεφ. ζ'.]

1. Περὶ δὲ τοῦ βαπτίσματος, οὕτω βαπτίσατε· ταῦτα πάντα προειπόντες, βαπτίσατε εἰς τὸ ὄνομα τοῦ Πατρός καὶ τοῦ Υἱοῦ καὶ τοῦ ἁγίου Πνεύματος ἐν ὕδατι ζῶντι.

2. Ἐὰν δὲ μὴ ἔχῃς ὕδωρ ζῶν, εἰς ἄλλο ὕδωρ βάπτισον· εἰ δ' οὐ δύνασαι ἐν ψυχρῷ, ἐν θερμῷ.

3. Ἐὰν δὲ ἀμφότερα μὴ ἔχῃς, ἔκχεον εἰς τὴν κεφαλὴν τρὶς ὕδωρ εἰς ὄνομα Πατρὸς καὶ Υἱοῦ καὶ ἁγίου Πνεύματος.

4. Πρὸ δὲ τοῦ βαπτίσματος προνηστευσάτω ὁ βαπτίζων καὶ ὁ βαπτιζόμενος καὶ εἴ τινες ἄλλοι δύνανται· κελεύεις ᵇ δὲ νηστεῦσαι τὸν βαπτιζόμενον πρὸ μιᾶς ἢ δύο.

ʳ [ἐπειδή, HL.]   ᵇ [κελεύσεις, B. &c.]

[CHAP. VI.]

1. Take heed that no one make thee to err from this way of teaching, since he teacheth thee not according to God.

2. For if indeed thou art able to bear the whole yoke of the Lord thou shalt be perfect, but if thou art not able, do what thou canst.

3. But concerning food, bear what thou canst, but beware exceedingly of that P offered to idols, for it is a service of dead gods.

[CHAP. VII.]

1. But concerning baptism, baptize thus: Having said [taught] beforehand all these things, baptize ye in the name of the Father, and of the Son, and of the Holy Ghost, in living water.

2. But if thou hast not living water, baptize in other water; and if thou canst not in cold, then in warm.

3. But if thou have not either, pour water thrice upon the head in the name of the Father, and of the Son, and of the Holy Ghost.

4. But before the baptism let him that baptizeth and him that is baptized fast, and any others who can; but thou shalt bid him that is baptized fast one or two days before.

P Cf. Acts xv. 29.

[Κεφ. η΄.]

1. Αἱ δὲ νηστεῖαι ὑμῶν μὴ ἔστωσαν μετὰ τῶν ὑποκριτῶν· νηστεύουσι γὰρ δευτέρᾳ σαββάτων καὶ πέμπτῃ· ὑμεῖς δὲ νηστεύσατε τετράδα καὶ παρασκευήν.

2. Μηδὲ προσεύχεσθε ὡς οἱ ὑποκριταί, ἀλλ᾽ ὡς ἐκέλευσεν ὁ Κύριος ἐν τῷ εὐαγγελίῳ αὐτοῦ οὕτως προσεύχεσθε· Πάτερ ἡμῶν ὁ ἐν τῷ οὐρανῷ, ἁγιασθήτω τὸ ὄνομά σου, ἐλθέτω ἡ βασιλεία σου, γεννηθήτω[1] τὸ θέλημά σου ὡς ἐν οὐρανῷ καὶ ἐπὶ γῆς. τὸν ἄρτον ἡμῶν τὸν ἐπιούσιον δὸς ἡμῖν σήμερον, καὶ ἄφες ἡμῖν τὴν ὀφειλὴν ἡμῶν ὡς καὶ ἡμεῖς ἀφίεμεν τοῖς ὀφειλέταις ἡμῶν, καὶ μὴ εἰσενέγκῃς ἡμᾶς εἰς πειρασμόν, ἀλλὰ ῥῦσαι ἡμᾶς ἀπὸ τοῦ πονηροῦ· ὅτι σοῦ ἐστιν ἡ δύναμις καὶ ἡ δόξα εἰς τοὺς αἰῶνας.

3. Τρὶς τῆς ἡμέρας οὕτω προσεύχεσθε.

[Κεφ. θ΄.]

1. Περὶ δὲ τῆς εὐχαριστίας, οὕτω[a] εὐχαριστήσατε·

2. Πρῶτον περὶ τοῦ ποτηρίου· Εὐχαριστοῦμέν σοι, Πάτερ ἡμῶν, ὑπὲρ τῆς ἁγίας ἀμπέλου Δαβὶδ τοῦ παιδός σου, ἧς ἐγνώρισας ἡμῖν διὰ Ἰησοῦ τοῦ παιδός σου· σοὶ ἡ δόξα εἰς τοὺς αἰῶνας.

3. Περὶ δὲ τοῦ κλάσματος· Εὐχαριστοῦμέν σοι, Πάτερ ἡμῶν, ὑπὲρ τῆς ζωῆς καὶ γνώσεως, ἧς ἐγνώρισας ἡμῖν διὰ Ἰησοῦ τοῦ παιδός σου· σοὶ ἡ δόξα εἰς τοὺς αἰῶνας.

[1] [γενηθήτω, B., &c.]   [a] [οὕτως, B., &c.]

[CHAP. VIII.]

1. But let not your fasts be together with the hypocrites, for they fast on the second and fifth days of the week, but ye shall fast the fourth day, and the preparation (Friday).

2. Neither pray ye as the hypocrites, but as the Lord commanded in His Gospel thus pray ye; "Our Father ⁹, which art in heaven, hallowed be Thy Name, Thy Kingdom come, Thy will be done in earth as it is in heaven, Give us this day our daily bread, And forgive us our debt as we forgive our debtors, And lead us not into temptation, but deliver us from evil, For Thine is the power and the glory for ever."

3. Pray thus thrice a day.

[CHAP. IX.]

1. But with regard to the Giving-of-thanks, give thanks after this manner.

2. First, with regard to the Cup, "We give thanks to Thee, our Father, for the holy vine of Thy child David, which Thou hast made known to us through Thy child Jesus; to Thee be glory for ever."

3. But with regard to the broken bread, "We give thanks to Thee, our Father, for the life and knowledge which Thou hast made known to us through Thy child Jesus; to Thee be glory for ever.

⁹ Matt. vi. 5—13.

4. Ὥσπερ ἦν τοῦτο κλάσμα διεσκορπισμένον ἐπάνω τῶν ὀρέων καὶ συναχθὲν ἐγένετο ἕν, οὕτω συναχθήτω σου ἡ ἐκκλησία ἀπὸ τῶν περάτων τῆς γῆς εἰς τὴν σὴν βασιλείαν· ὅτι σοῦ ἐστιν ἡ δόξα καὶ ἡ δύναμις διὰ Ἰησοῦ Χριστοῦ εἰς τοὺς αἰῶνας.

5. Μηδεὶς δὲ φαγέτω μηδὲ πιέτω ἀπὸ τῆς εὐχαριστίας ὑμῶν, ἀλλ' οἱ βαπτισθέντες εἰς ὄνομα Κυρίου· καὶ γὰρ περὶ τούτου εἴρηκεν ὁ Κύριος· Μὴ δῶτε τὸ ἅγιον τοῖς κυσί.

[Κεφ. ι'.]

1. Μετὰ δὲ τὸ ἐμπλησθῆναι οὕτως εὐχαριστήσατε·

2. Εὐχαριστοῦμέν σοι, Πάτερ ἅγιε, ὑπὲρ τοῦ ἁγίου ὀνόματός σου, οὗ κατεσκήνωσας ἐν ταῖς καρδίαις ὑμῶν[x] καὶ ὑπὲρ τῆς γνώσεως καὶ πίστεως καὶ ἀθανασίας, ἧς ἐγνώρισας ἡμῖν διὰ Ἰησοῦ τοῦ παιδός σου· σοὶ ἡ δόξα εἰς τοὺς αἰῶνας.

3. Σύ, δέσποτα παντοκράτορ, ἔκτισας τὰ πάντα ἕνεκεν τοῦ ὀνόματός σου, τροφήν τε καὶ ποτὸν ἔδωκας τοῖς ἀνθρώποις εἰς ἀπόλαυσιν ἵνα σοι εὐχαριστήσωσιν, ἡμῖν δὲ ἐχαρίσω πνευματικὴν τροφὴν καὶ ποτὸν καὶ ζωὴν αἰώνιον διὰ τοῦ παιδός σου.

4. Πρὸ πάντων εὐχαριστοῦμέν σοι ὅτι δυνατὸς εἶ σύ[y]· ἡ δόξα εἰς τοὺς αἰῶνας.

[x] [ἡμῶν, B., &c.]   [y] [σοὶ, Hr. et, om. σύ, B. Hl.]

4. "As this broken bread was scattered upon the mountains and gathered together became one, so let Thy Church be gathered together from the ends of the earth into Thy kingdom, for Thine is the glory and the power through Jesus Christ for ever."

5. But let no one eat or drink of your Eucharist except those baptized in the name of the Lord, for regarding this also the Lord hath said, "Give not that which is holy to the dogs ʳ."

[CHAP. X.]

1. But after being filled, give thanks thus.

2. We give thanks to Thee, Holy Father, for Thy holy Name, which Thou hast caused to dwell in our hearts, and for the knowledge and faith and immortality which Thou hast made known to us by Jesus Thy Child, to Thee be glory for ever.

3. Thou, O Almighty Ruler, madest all things for Thy Name's sake; Thou gavest men food and drink for enjoyment that they might give thanks to Thee, but us Thou blessedst with spiritual food and drink and eternal life through Thy Child.

4. Before all things we give thanks to Thee that Thou art mighty; to Thee be glory for ever.

ʳ Matt. vii. 6.

5. Μνήσθητι, Κύριε, τῆς ἐκκλησίας σου τοῦ ῥύσασθαι αὐτὴν ἀπὸ παντὸς πονηροῦ καὶ τελειῶσαι αὐτὴν ἐν τῇ ἀγάπῃ σου, καὶ σύναξον αὐτὴν ἀπὸ τῶν τεσσάρων ἀνέμων τὴν ἁγιασθεῖσαν εἰς τὴν σὴν βασιλείαν, ἣν ἡτοίμασας αὐτῇ· ὅτι σοῦ ἐστιν ἡ δύναμις καὶ ἡ δόξα εἰς τοὺς αἰῶνας.

6. Ἐλθέτω χάρις καὶ παρελθέτω ὁ κόσμος οὗτος. Ὡς ἀννὰ^z τῷ θεῷ^a Δαβίδ. Εἴ τις ἅγιός ἐστιν, ἐρχέσθω. εἴ τις οὐκ ἔστι, μετανοείτω· μαραναθά. Ἀμήν.

7. Τοῖς δὲ προφήταις ἐπιτρέπετε εὐχαριστεῖν ὅσα θέλουσιν.

[Κεφ. ια'.]

1. Ὃς ἂν οὖν ἐλθὼν διδάξῃ ὑμᾶς ταῦτα πάντα τὰ προειρημένα, δέξασθε αὐτόν·

2. Ἐὰν δὲ αὐτὸς ὁ διδάσκων στραφεὶς διδάσκῃ ἄλλην διδαχὴν εἰς τὸ καταλῦσαι, μὴ αὐτοῦ ἀκούσητε· εἰς δὲ τὸ προσθεῖναι δικαιοσύνην καὶ γνῶσιν Κυρίου, δέξασθε αὐτὸν ὡς Κύριον.

3. Περὶ δὲ τῶν ἀποστόλων καὶ προφητῶν κατὰ τὸ δόγμα τοῦ εὐαγγελίου οὕτως ποιήσατε.

4. Πᾶς δὲ ἀπόστολος ἐρχόμενος πρὸς ὑμᾶς δεχθήτω ὡς Κύριος·

5. Οὐ^b μενεῖ δὲ ἡμέραν μίαν, ἐὰν δὲ ᾖ χρεία, καὶ τὴν ἄλλην· τρεῖς δὲ ἐὰν μείνῃ, ψευδοπροφήτης ἐστίν.

---

^z [Ὡσαννά.]   ^a [υἱῷ, B. Hl.]
^b [οὐ, om. Hl. ; οὐ μενεῖ δὲ εἰ μὴ, Hr. ; οὔ, Zahn.]

5. Remember, O Lord, Thy Church to deliver her from all evil and to perfect her in Thy love, and gather her together from the four winds ', her the sanctified, into Thy kingdom which Thou preparedst for her; for Thine is the power and the glory for ever.

6. Let grace come, and let this world pass away. Hosanna to the God of David. If any one be holy let him come, if any one be not holy let him repent. Maranatha. Amen.

7. But suffer the prophets to give thanks as much as [i.e. in what words] they will.

[CHAP. XI.]

1. Whosoever therefore cometh and teacheth you all the things aforesaid, receive him.

2. But if the teacher himself being perverted teacheth another teaching to the undoing [thereof], hear him not, but if [his teaching be] to the increasing of righteousness and the knowledge of the Lord, receive him as the Lord.

3. But with regard to the apostles and prophets, according to the command of the Gospel, so do ye.

4. Let every apostle that cometh to you be received as the Lord ᵗ.

5. But he shall not remain [more than] one day, and if there be necessity the second also, but if he remain three days he is a false prophet.

' Matt. xxiv. 31.   ᵗ Ibid. x. 40.

6. Ἐξερχόμενος δὲ ὁ ἀπόστολος μηδὲν λαμβα-
νέτω εἰ μὴ ἄρτον ἕως οὗ αὐλισθῇ. ἐὰν δὲ ἀργύριον
αἰτῇ, ψευδοπροφήτης ἐστί.

7. Καὶ πάντα προφήτην λαλοῦντα ἐν πνεύματι
οὐ πειράσετε οὐδὲ διακρινεῖτε· πᾶσα γὰρ ἁμαρτία
ἀφεθήσεται, αὕτη δὲ ἡ ἁμαρτία οὐκ ἀφεθήσεται.

8. Οὐ πᾶς δὲ ὁ λαλῶν ἐν πνεύματι προφήτης
ἐστίν, ἀλλ᾽ ἐὰν ἔχῃ τοὺς τρόπους Κυρίου. Ἀπὸ
οὖν τῶν τρόπων γνωσθήσεται ὁ ψευδοπροφήτης
καὶ ὁ προφήτης.

9. Καὶ πᾶς προφήτης ὁρίζων τράπεζαν ἐν πνεύματι οὐ φάγεται ἀπ᾽ αὐτῆς, εἰδὲ μήγε ψευδοπροφήτης ἐστί.

10. Πᾶς δὲ προφήτης διδάσκων τὴν ἀλήθειαν,
εἰ ἃ διδάσκει οὐ ποιεῖ, ψευδοπροφήτης ἐστί.

11. Πᾶς δὲ προφήτης δεδοκιμασμένος ἀληθινὸς
ποιῶν[c] εἰς μυστήριον κοσμικὸν[d] ἐκκλησίας, μὴ
διδάσκων δὲ ποιεῖν ὅσα αὐτὸς ποιεῖ, οὐ κριθήσεται
ἐφ᾽ ὑμῶν· μετὰ Θεοῦ γὰρ ἔχει τὴν κρίσιν· ὡσαύτως
γὰρ ἐποίησαν καὶ οἱ ἀρχαῖοι προφῆται.

12. Ὃς δ᾽ ἂν εἴπῃ ἐν πνεύματι· Δός μοι ἀργύ-
ρια ἢ ἕτερά τινα, οὐκ ἀκούσεσθε αὐτοῦ· ἐὰν δὲ
περὶ ἄλλων ὑστερούντων εἴπῃ δοῦναι, μηδεὶς αὐτὸν
κρινέτω.

[Κεφ. ιβ΄.]

1. Πᾶς δὲ ὁ ἐρχόμενος ἐν ὀνόματι Κυρίου δεχθήτω, ἔπειτα δὲ δοκιμάσαντες αὐτὸν γνώσεσθε,
σύνεσιν γὰρ ἕξεται[e], δεξιὰν καὶ ἀριστεράν.

---

[c] [μνῶν, Hl.]   [d] [κοσμικῶν, Hl.]   [e] [ἕξετε, B., &c.]

6. And when the apostle departeth let him take nothing except bread [to last] till he reach his lodging. But if he ask for money he is a false prophet.

7. And no prophet that speaketh in the Spirit shall ye try or prove, for every sin shall be forgiven, but this sin shall not be forgiven.

8. Not every one that speaketh in the spirit is a prophet but only if he have the behaviour of the Lord. By their behaviour then shall the false prophet and the prophet be known.

9. And no prophet that ordereth a table in the spirit eateth of it except he be a false prophet.

10. And every prophet that teacheth the truth if he doeth not what he teacheth is a false prophet.

11. And every approved true prophet, who maketh assemblies for a worldly mystery, but teacheth not to do such things as he himself doeth, shall not be judged of you, for he hath his judgment with God, for likewise did also the ancient prophets.

12. But whosoever saith in the spirit, Give me money or any other things, ye shall not hearken to him, but if he bid to give for others that lack, let no one judge him.

[CHAP. XII.]

1. But let every one that cometh in the Name of the Lord be received, and then proving him ye shall know the right and left [true and false *], for ye shall have understanding.

* Or, see Note, p. 108.

2. Εἰ μὲν παρόδιός ἐστιν ὁ ἐρχόμενος, βοηθεῖτε αὐτῷ ὅσον δύνασθε· οὐ μενεῖ δὲ πρὸς ὑμᾶς εἰ μὴ δύο ἢ τρεῖς ἡμέρας, ἐὰν ᾖ ἀνάγκη.

3. Εἰ δὲ θέλει πρὸς ὑμᾶς καθῆσαι[f], τεχνίτης ὤν, ἐργαζέσθω καὶ φαγέτω·

4. Εἰ δὲ οὐκ ἔχει τέχνην, κατὰ τὴν σύνεσιν ὑμῶν προνοήσατε, πῶς μὴ ἀργὸς μεθ᾽ ὑμῶν ζήσεται χριστιανός.

5. Εἰ δ᾽ οὐ θέλει οὕτω ποιεῖν, χριστέμπορός ἐστιν· προσέχετε ἀπὸ τῶν τοιούτων.

[Κεφ. ιγʹ.]

1. Πᾶς δὲ προφήτης ἀληθινός, θέλων καθῆσαι[g] πρὸς ὑμᾶς, ἄξιός ἐστι τῆς τροφῆς αὐτοῦ.

2. Ὡσαύτως διδάσκαλος ἀληθινός ἐστιν ἄξιος καὶ αὐτός ὥσπερ ὁ ἐργάτης τῆς τροφῆς αὐτοῦ·

3. Πᾶσαν οὖν ἀπαρχὴν γεννημάτων ληνοῦ καὶ ἅλωνος βοῶν τε καὶ προβάτων λαβὼν δώσεις τὴν ἀπαρχὴν τοῖς προφήταις· αὐτοὶ γάρ εἰσιν οἱ ἀρχιερεῖς ὑμῶν.

4. Ἐὰν δὲ μὴ ἔχητε προφήτην, δότε τοῖς πτωχοῖς·

5. Ἐὰν σιτίαν ποιῇς, τὴν ἀπαρχὴν λαβὼν δὸς κατὰ τὴν ἐντολήν·

6. Ὡσαύτως κεράμιον οἴνου ἢ ἐλαίου ἀνοίξας, τὴν ἀπαρχὴν λαβὼν δὸς τοῖς προφήταις.

---

[f] [καθίσαι, Hr. Hl.]   [g] [καθίσαι, Hr. Hl.]

2. If indeed he that cometh is a wayfarer help him as much as ye can, but he shall not remain with you longer than two or three days unless there be necessity.

3. But if he willeth to settle among you and is a craftsman, let him work and [so] eat.

4. But if he have no craft, according to your understanding provide that a Christian shall live with you without being idle.

5. But if he will not act thus he is one who maketh merchandize of Christ; Beware of such.

[Chap. XIII.]

1. But every true prophet that willeth to settle among you is worthy of his meat.

2. Likewise a true teacher is himself worthy, like the workman, of his meat [v].

3. Therefore all the firstfruits of the produce of press and floor, of oxen and sheep, thou shalt take and give to the prophets for they are your chief priests.

4. But if ye have not a prophet give to the poor.

5. If thou preparest bread, take the firstfruits and give according to the commandment.

6. Likewise when thou openest a jar of wine or of oil, take the firstfruits and give to the prophets.

[v] Matt. x. 10.

7. Ἀργυρίου δὲ καὶ ἱματισμοῦ καὶ παντὸς κτήματος λαβὼν τὴν ἀπαρχὴν ὡς ἄν σοι δόξῃ, δὸς
κατὰ τὴν ἐντολήν.

[Κεφ. ιδ´.]

1. Κατὰ κυριακὴν δὲ Κυρίου συναχθέντες κλά-
σατε ἄρτον καὶ εὐχαριστήσατε προσεξομολογησ-
άμενοι[h] τὰ παραπτώματα ὑμῶν, ὅπως καθαρὰ ἡ
θυσία ἡμῶν ᾖ.

2. Πᾶς δὲ ἔχων τὴν[i] ἀμφιβολίαν μετὰ τοῦ ἑταίρου αὐτοῦ μὴ συνελθέτω ὑμῖν ἕως οὗ διαλλαγῶσιν,
ἵνα μὴ κοινωθῇ ἡ θυσία ἡμῶν[k].

3. Αὕτη γάρ ἐστιν ἡ ῥηθεῖσα ὑπὸ Κυρίου· Ἐν
παντὶ τόπῳ καὶ χρόνῳ προσφέρειν μοι θυσίαν
καθαράν· ὅτι βασιλεὺς μέγας εἰμί, λέγει Κύριος,
καὶ τὸ ὄνομά μου θαυμαστὸν ἐν τοῖς ἔθνεσι.

[Κεφ. ιε´.]

1. Χειροτονήσατε οὖν ἑαυτοῖς ἐπισκόπους καὶ
διακόνους ἀξίους τοῦ Κυρίου, ἄνδρας πραεῖς καὶ
ἀφιλαργύρους καὶ ἀληθεῖς καὶ δεδοκιμασμένους·
ὑμῖν γὰρ λειτουργοῦσι καὶ αὐτοὶ τὴν λειτουργίαν
τῶν προφητῶν καὶ διδασκάλων.

2. Μὴ οὖν ὑπερίδητε αὐτούς· αὐτοὶ γάρ εἰσιν οἱ
τετιμημένοι ὑμῶν μετὰ τῶν προφητῶν καὶ διδασκάλων.

[h] [προεξομ. Hl.]   [i] [τινά, Hr.]   [k] [ὑμῶν, B, &c.]

7. And of silver, and raiment, and every possession, take the firstfruits as seemeth good to thee, and give according to the commandment.

[CHAP. XIV.]

1. And on the Lord's Day of the Lord come together and break bread, and give thanks after confessing your transgressions, that your sacrifice may be pure.

2. Let no one that hath a dispute with his fellow come together with you until they be reconciled, that your sacrifice may not be defiled [w].

3. For this is that which was spoken by the Lord, "In every place and time offer Me a pure sacrifice, for I am a great King, saith the Lord, and My Name is wonderful among the Gentiles [x]."

[CHAP. XV.]

1. Elect therefore for yourselves bishops and deacons worthy of the Lord, men meek, and not lovers of money, and truthful, and approved, for they too minister to you the ministry of the prophets and teachers.

2. Therefore despise them not, for they are those that are honoured of you with the prophets and teachers.

[w] Cf. Matt. v. 23, 24.   [x] Mal. i. 11, 14.

3. Ἐλέγχετε δὲ ἀλλήλους μὴ ἐν ὀργῇ ἀλλ' ἐν
εἰρήνῃ, ὡς ἔχετε ἐν τῷ εὐαγγελίῳ· καὶ παντὶ ἀστο-
χοῦντι κατὰ τοῦ ἑτέρου μηδεὶς λαλείτω μηδὲ παρ
ὑμῶν ἀκουέτω[1], ἕως οὗ μετανοήσῃ.

4. Τὰς δὲ εὐχὰς ὑμῶν καὶ τὰς ἐλεημοσύνας καὶ
πάσας τὰς πράξεις οὕτως ποιήσατε ὡς ἔχετε ἐν τῷ
εὐαγγελίῳ τοῦ Κυρίου ἡμῶν.

[Κεφ. ις΄.]

1. Γρηγορεῖτε ὑπὲρ τῆς ζωῆς ὑμῶν· οἱ λύχνοι
ὑμῶν μὴ σβεσθήτωσαν, καὶ αἱ ὀσφύες ὑμῶν μὴ
ἐκλυέσθωσαν, ἀλλὰ γίνεσθε ἕτοιμοι· οὐ γὰρ οἴδατε
τὴν ὥραν ἐν ᾗ ὁ Κύριος ἡμῶν ἔρχεται.

2. Πυκνῶς δὲ συναχθήσεσθε ζητοῦντες τὰ ἀνήκοντα ταῖς ψυχαῖς ὑμῶν. οὐ γὰρ ὠφελήσει ὑμᾶς ὁ
πᾶς χρόνος τῆς πίστεως ὑμῶν ἐὰν μὴ ἐν τῷ ἐσχάτῳ
καιρῷ τελειωθῆτε.

3. Ἐν γὰρ ταῖς ἐσχάταις ἡμέραις πληθυνθήσονται οἱ ψευδοπροφῆται καὶ οἱ φθορεῖς καὶ στρα-
φήσονται τὰ πρόβατα εἰς λύκους καὶ ἡ ἀγάπη
στραφήσεται εἰς μῖσος.

4. Αὐξανούσης γὰρ τῆς ἀνομίας μισήσουσιν
ἀλλήλους καὶ διώξουσι καὶ παραδώσουσι, καὶ τότε
φανήσεται ὁ κοσμοπλάνος ὡς υἱὸς Θεοῦ καὶ ποιήσει
σημεῖα καὶ τέρατα, καὶ ἡ γῆ παραδοθήσεται εἰς
χεῖρας αὐτοῦ, καὶ ποιήσει ἀθέμιτα ἃ οὐδέποτε
γέγονεν ἐξ αἰῶνος.

[1] [ἀκουέσθω, H1.]

3. But reprove one another not in wrath but in peace, as ye have it in the Gospel, and with every one that trangresseth against his neighbour let no one speak, nor let him hear [a word] from you until he repent.

4. But your prayers and alms and all your actions so do as ye have it in the Gospel of our Lord.

[CHAP. XVI.]

1. Watch over your life, let not your lamps be quenched and let not your loins be ungirded, but be ye ready, for ye know not the hour in which your Lord cometh [y].

2. But be ye frequently gathered together, seeking the things that are profitable for your souls, for the whole time of your faith shall not profit you except in the last season ye be [already] perfect.

3. For in the last days shall the false prophets and destroyers be multiplied, and the sheep shall be turned to wolves, and love shall be turned to hate.

4. For when lawlessness increaseth, they shall hate and persecute, and deliver up one another; and then shall appear the deceiver of the world as God's Son, and shall do signs and wonders [z], and the earth shall be delivered into his hands, and he shall commit iniquities which have never yet been from the beginning of the world.

[y] Cf. Matt. xxv. 13.   [z] Cf. Matt. xxiv. 24, Acts ii. 19.

5. Τότε ἥξει ἡ κτίσις τῶν ἀνθρώπων εἰς τὴν ϝύρωσιν τῆς δοκιμασίας καὶ σκανδαλισθήσονται πολλοὶ καὶ ἀπολοῦνται, οἱ δὲ ὑπομείναντες ἐν τῇ πίστει αὐτῶν σωθήσονται ὑπ᾽ ᵐ αὐτοῦ τοῦ καταθέματος.

6. Καὶ τότε φανήσεται τὰ σημεῖα τῆς ἀληθείας· πρῶτον σημεῖον ἐκπετάσεως ἐν οὐρανῷ, εἶτα σημεῖον φωνῆς σάλπιγγος, καὶ τὸ τρίτον ἀνάστασις νεκρῶν·

7. Οὐ πάντων δέ, ἀλλ᾽ ὡς ἐρρέθη· Ἥξει ὁ Κύριος καὶ πάντες οἱ ἅγιοι μετ᾽ αὐτοῦ.

8. Τότε ὄψεται ὁ κόσμος τὸν Κύριον ἐρχόμενον ἐπάνω τῶν νεφελῶν τοῦ οὐρανοῦ.

ᵐ [ἀπ᾽, Hl.]

5. And then shall the race of men come into the fire of testing, and many shall be offended and perish, but they who endure in their faith shall be saved under the curse itself.

6. And then shall appear the signs of the truth, first the sign of opening in heaven, then the sign of the voice of the trumpet, and the third, the resurrection of the dead.

7. Not, however, of all, but as was said, " The Lord shall come, and all the saints with Him [a]."

8. Then shall the world see the Lord coming upon the clouds of heaven.

[a] Zech. xiv. 5.

NOTES.

The Title. It seems strange to find a book with two differing titles, neither of which corresponds with those used by other writers* in speaking of what is undoubtedly the same work. The second is most likely the older, because fuller, and may not improbably be original, and the mention of the twelve Apostles points to a time when, as in the body of the writing, the title Apostle was not confined to those subsequently called " The Twelve."

τοῖς ἔθνεσιν. Not Gentiles as distinguished from the Jews, but as those included in our Lord's charge μαθητεύσατε πάντα τὰ ἔθνη. Matt. xxviii. 19.

I. 2. ἀγαπήσεις κ.τ.λ. It is unfortunate that the writer did not complete his teaching in this verse by mentioning the Atonement; as is done in Ep. Barn. c. 18, ἀγαπ. τὸν Θ. τον ποιήσ. σε ἐξ ὅλης τῆς καρδίας σου, καὶ δοξάσεις τὸν λυτρωσάμενόν σε ἐκ θανάτου. If the Διδαχή copied Barnabas, would such a clause as this have been dropped out? It is more likely that the second clause

---

* *Euseb. H. E.* iii. 25 ; τῶν ἀποστόλων αἱ λεγόμεναι διδαχαί. *Athanas. Fest. Ep.* 39 ; διδαχὴ καλουμένη τῶν ἀποστόλων. *Synopsis S. Scripturæ,* ascribed to Athanasius; διδαχὴ ἀποστόλων. *Anastasius Sinaita, Quæst. et Resp. ;* διδαχαὶ τῶν ἀποστόλων. *Nicephorus Stichometria;* διδαχὴ ἀποστόλων. *Pseudo-Cyprian de Aleatoribus* perhaps refers by Doctrinæ Apostolorum to this work; *St. Clement of Alexandria* quotes the work as Scripture: see note on III. 5.

is an addition by a later hand in course of working up existing material, than that a copyist
should have omitted it.

‿ 3. νηστεύετε. Comp. Matt. xvii. 21; Mark ix. 29.
The modern depreciation of fasting is neither
Scriptural nor primitive. In the passages referred to, our Lord seems to point to a special
energy and power gained by fasting. And so in
this passage there may be an ascending scale.
Return good words for evil, pray for those who
bear you ill-will, fast for those who actively persecute you.

4. σαρκικῶν καὶ σωματικῶν. The MS. reading has
been changed by all editors except Harnack into
κοσμικῶν, which latter occurs in the parallel passage of the Ap. Const., and is supported by
1 Pet. ii. 11, and 2 Clem. xvii.

ἐάν τίς σοι δῷ κ.τ.λ. The following passage may
be founded on Matt. v. 39—41; Luke vi. 29, 30.
The writer, in his quotations, often varies from
the text of our Evangelists, or mixes St. Matthew
and St. Luke together. Harnack points out a
similarity between this passage and Tatian's Diatessaron, which gives the clauses in exactly the
order of the Διδαχή. Tatian lived, however, in
the second century, at a date later than that of
the work before us. Was there some kind of
"Gospel" current, perhaps orally, not the same
as that of any one of our four Evangelists?

οὐδὲ γὰρ δύνασαι. This may be simply a statement of the fact that the person who uses vio-
lence is the stronger, which would, however, be
a weak close to the paragraph. It is probably

a reference to our Lord's commandment in the Sermon on the Mount on which the passage is founded. Bryennius quotes a passage from St. John Climacus as follows: εὐσεβῶν μὲν τῷ αἰτοῦντι διδόναι, εὐσεβεστέρων δὲ καὶ τῷ μὴ αἰτοῦντι· τὸ δὲ ἀπὸ τοῦ αἴροντος μὴ ἀπαιτεῖν, δυναμένους μάλιστα, τάχα τῶν ἀπαθῶν καὶ μονῶν ἴδιον καθέστηκεν. Migne, Gr., lxxxviii. p. 1029. But the passage may possibly be taken with what follows, that what is once given, even if improperly, no longer belongs to the giver. He may not ask for it back, but must leave the matter to a higher power.

6. ἀλλὰ καὶ περὶ τούτου κ.τ.λ. This seems in contradiction to what has gone before, but possibly only refers to the case of good grounds for suspicion as to the worthiness of the recipient. The copyist (Const. Ap. vii. 1) omits the passage. So long as promiscuous charity was the rule, there would always be risk of impostors being relieved at the cost of the deserving. Hence the later rule of giving alms by means of the bishop, who, with his assistants, would know of fit cases for relief.

ἱδρωτάτω [—σάτω], a somewhat strange expression; possibly Hilgenfeld's suggestion ἱδρυσάτω should be accepted. There is absolutely no clue as to whence the passage is taken. With the argument of this passage may be compared the teaching of the Apostolical Constitutions, iv. 2, 3: καὶ γὰρ ἀληθῶς μακάριός ἐστιν ὃς ἂν δυνάμενος βοηθεῖν ἑαυτῷ μὴ θλίβῃ τόπον ὀρφανοῦ, ξένου τε καὶ χήρας· ἐπεὶ καὶ ὁ Κύριος μακάριον εἶπεν εἶναι τὸν διδόντα ἤ περ τὸν λαμβάνοντα. Καὶ γὰρ εἴρηται πάλιν ὑπ᾽ αὐτοῦ, Οὐαὶ τοῖς ἔχουσι καὶ ἐν ὑποκρίσει λαμβάνουσιν ἤ δυναμένοις

βοηθεῖν ἑαυτοῖς καὶ λαμβάνειν παρ' ἑτέρων βουλομένοις
.... ὁ δὲ ἔχων καὶ ἐν ὑποκρίσει λαμβάνων ἢ δι' ἀργίαν
ἀντὶ τοῦ ἐργαζόμενον βοηθεῖν καὶ ἑτέροις, δίκην ὀφλήσει
τῷ Θεῷ, ὅτι πενήτων ἥρπασε ψωμόν.

II. 5. μεμεστωμένος πράξει, cf. Matt. xxiii. 3. The reference evidently is to much talking but little
performance, activity in good works being the
complement without which talk is vain.

7. All men are divided into three classes: 1. Sin-
ners who may be rebuked; 2. Such as reject ad-
monition and are to be prayed for; 3. The faithful. Of the twenty-five points of warning in
this chapter, the first ten refer to the Commandments of the second table, the rest mostly to
sins of the tongue, specially to those against
charity.

III. 4. περικαθαίρων. This word is used Deut. xviii.
10, for "making to pass" through the fire. It
must refer here to all kinds of heathen purifications and lustrations, whether by fire or water.

5. ὁδηγεῖ τὸ ψεῦσμα κ.τ.λ. This is the passage quoted
by Clement, Strom. I., as Scripture, οὗτος κλέπτης
ὑπὸ τῆς γραφῆς εἴρηται· φησὶ γοῦν· υἱέ, μὴ γίνου ψεύσ-
της· ὁδηγεῖ γὰρ τὸ ψεῦσμα πρὸς τὴν κλοπήν. Migne,
Gr., viii. 818.

IV. This chapter contains various moral precepts af-
fecting Christians as members of the Church,
rather than as previously in their individual
capacity.

1. ἡ κυριότης, a somewhat curious phrase, and one
which cannot be translated so as to give its full
meaning in English. In Ap. Const. vii. 9, the
passage is thus paraphrased. ὅπου γὰρ ἡ περὶ Θεοῦ

διδασκαλία, ἐκεῖ ὁ Θεὸς πάρεστιν. "For where is the
teaching concerning God, there God is present."
κυριότης λαλεῖται is a wide expression implying a
large amount of possible instruction. It would
cover a whole Christology.

4. οὐ διψυχήσεις. Harnack refers this doubt to the
last judgment, but it is difficult to see why; also,
as he says, all later compilers who have used this
work understand it of hearing prayer, as e.g. Ap.
Const. vii. 11, οὐ διψυχήσεις ἐν προσευχῇ σου.
Bryennius compares Ecclus. i. 28 ; comp. also
such passages as Matt. xxi. 22 ; 1 John v. 14, 15.

6. ἐὰν ἔχῃς. Comp. besides reff. 2 Clemens Rom.
xvi., where almsgiving is spoken of as κούφισμα
ἁμαρτίας.

10. οὐκ ἐπιτάξεις. Compare Ephes. vi. 9, where St.
Paul teaches how masters should treat their slaves,
"forbearing threatening, knowing that your [καὶ
αὐτῶν καὶ ὑμῶν] Master also is in heaven ; neither
is there respect of persons [προσωποληψία] with
Him." The teaching of universal brotherhood
and equality eliminated first the worst points in
slavery, and gradually slavery itself; but the work
being deep and thorough was necessarily slow.

τὸ πνεῦμα. The only mention in this treatise,
except ch. vii. in the baptismal form, of the
Holy Ghost. Harnack compares Rom. viii. 29, 30.

14. ἐν ἐκκλησίᾳ. Except so far as James v. 16 is
parallel, this is the earliest mention of confession of sins in the church or congregation, and
is therefore a valuable and interesting historical
point.

V. This chapter is almost word for word the same

as Barn. Ep. xx., and may also be compared with Hermas, Mand. viii.

VI. 1. There would seem to be no reason for referring this passage, if indeed any of the Διδαχή, as suggested by Hilgenfeld, to Montanistic tendencies on the part of the writer: Harnack's quotation from Hermas, Mand. xii. c. 3, 4, that the Commandments can hardly be kept, διότι σκληραί εἰσι λίαν, is completely modified by the sequel which he omits, ἀποκριθεὶς λέγει μοι, Ἐὰν σὺ σεαυτῷ προθῆς ὅτι δύνανται φυλαχθῆναι, εὐκόπως αὐτὰς φυλάξεις, καὶ οὐκ ἔσονται σκληραί, κ.τ.λ.

There would seem rather to be a reminiscence of our Lord's words, "All men cannot receive this saying," Matt. xix. 11, and "If thou wilt be perfect," ib. 21; or of St. Paul, "Every man hath his proper gift of God," 1 Cor. vii. 6, 7, 25—28; and with regard to meats, some such feeling as that referred to by St. Paul, Rom. xiv. 2. The next verse with regard to meat offered to idols reads as though St. Paul's modification (1 Cor. viii. 4, and x. 19) of the injunction, Acts xv. 29, were unknown; but the same restriction is found in writers of the second century. Hilgenfeld quotes parallel passages, Theoph. ad Autol. i. 9, τὰ μὲν ὀνόματα ὧν φῆς σέβεσθαι Θεῶν ὀνόματά ἐστι νεκρῶν ἀνθρώπων; and Petri Prædic. (in Nov. Test. ext. Can.), p. 56, l. 35, τὰ ἴδια βρώματα βρωτοῖς θύματα θύουσιν καὶ νεκρὰ νεκροῖς προσφέροντες ὡς θεοῖς ἀχαριστοῦσι τῷ Θεῷ διὰ τούτων ἀρνούμενοι αὐτὸν εἶναι; and Harnack, a still more apposite passage, 2 Clem. iii. 1, ἡμεῖς οἱ ζῶντες τοῖς νεκροῖς θεοῖς οὐ θύομεν κ.τ.λ.

VII. 1. The preceding chapters contain such moral instruction as was considered necessary before baptism. Nothing has been said, however, as to any teaching about God and the Christian faith; nevertheless we need not conclude that the neophyte was taught nothing on such subjects, but rather that for some reason the writer of the Διδαχή, confining himself to practical matters alone, did not think fit to include what we should call dogmatic teaching in the scope of his work, but left it to be supplied orally by those who spoke the word of God and of the 'Lordship' of God, and by the saints whose words should refresh the hearer, (ch. iv. 1, 2). Moreover, such a statement as that in ch. iv. 10, that God calls only those "whom the Spirit hath prepared," would require some explanatory teaching. Compare conversely St. Philip and the Eunuch (Acts viii.), and St. Paul and the jailer at Philippi (Acts xvi. 31). There probably may, too, as Bryennius suggests, have been special reasons for enforcing the moral law : ἡ Διδαχὴ περὶ τούτων οὐδὲν εἶπεν ἰδίᾳ, ἅτε πρακτικὴ διδασκαλία οὖσα καὶ τὴν πρᾶξιν σκοποῦσα μάλιστα. Bryennius *in loc.*

The rules as to baptism are as clear as can be. The candidate having been instructed, is to be baptized in the name of the Father, of the Son, and of the Holy Ghost; if possible, in running water, doubtless in memory of our Lord's Baptism in the river Jordan. Should running water not be at hand, standing water will suffice, whether cold or warm, probably (according to a quotation in Bryennius from St. Gregory Nyssen) in case of sickness, or winter. So far, immersion seems to be contemplated; but we next meet, for the first time in ecclesiastical history, with express recognition of the sufficiency of affusion. If running water and standing water, as a lake or pond, are both wanting, "pour water thrice on the head in the name of the Father, of the Son, and of the Holy Ghost." This can hardly refer solely to clinical baptism, as the direction expressly relates to the quantity of water, not in any way to the state of the candidate.

Possibly ταῦτα πάντα προειπόντες may refer to some profession, or its equivalent immediately before baptism; while fasting is ordered before baptism for the baptizer and "any others who can," the candidate himself having also to fast for the fixed time of one or two days. This fast, as regards all but the candidate, seems to have fallen gradually into disuse; but see St. Chrysost. Sermo antequam iret in Exsil., Migne, Gr. iii. p. 431, Λέγουσί μοι, ὅτι ἔφαγες καὶ ἐβάπτισας. Εἰ ἐποίησα τοῦτο ἀνάθεμα ἔσομαι, κ.τ.λ. For the adult candidate the rule exists still in East and West; and possibly the rule in force in England till the Reformation, that the Bishop and candidates for Confirmation should be fasting, is a reminiscence of the old baptismal order.

VIII. In this chapter we have the earliest rules for Wednesday and Friday as fasting-days, instead of Monday and Thursday, shewing, with the later notice as to the Lord's day, how the Christian division of the week was taking root. After the

H

Council of Elvira, A.D. 305, Saturday came to be
observed in the West, and Wednesday gradually
dropped out. (Bingham, Ant., XXI. iii. 6.) The
designation of the Jews by the term "hypocrites"
is probably not so much a mark of personal feeling, which does not shew itself in the Διδαχή, as
an adaptation of our Lord's words, " When ye
fast, be not as the hypocrites," &c. (Matt. vi. 16);
and this view is supported by the repetition of
the word hypocrites in the directions for prayer,
where the application to the Jews would be simply
out of place.

1. ὑμεῖς δὲ νηστεύσατε κ.τ.λ. It would be interesting
to know whether the Wednesday and Friday fast
was originally connected with the events of our
Lord's Passion, or, as is here implied, in order to
avoid the Jewish fasting days, Monday and Thursday. St. Clement Alex., Strom. vii., says that
he who has true wisdom, οἶδεν καὶ τῆς νηστείας τὰ
αἰνίγματα τῶν ἡμερῶν τούτων, but refers only to the
heathen names of the days in explanation. Migne,
Gr. ix. 504.

παρασκευήν. The preparation for the Jewish
Sabbath [Matt. xxvii. 62, and parallel passages].
The name still remains in Greek service-books,
and in the Latin office for Good Friday, *Feria
sexta in Parasceve.*

2. The Lord's Prayer is the same form as that
given by St. Matthew, vi. 5—13, with the following exceptions, ἐν τῷ οὐρανῷ, the singular in place
of the plural, ἐν τοῖς οὐρανοῖς, in the invocation;
the omission of the article before γῆς in the third,

and τὴν ὀφειλὴν for τὰ ὀφειλήματα, in the fifth peti-
tion. . There seems to be no other authority for
these variations from the received text. The
doxology appears, but with the omission of the
words ἡ βασιλεία, which exist in all MSS. and
versions which have the doxology at all, with
the exception of one version, the Sahidic, which
fact Harnack acutely notes as supporting his view
as to the birthplace of the Διδαχή.

It may be noted that the Διδαχή supports ἀφίεμεν
of the received Text, against ἀφήκαμεν of Tischendorf, the Revisers, &c.; and ἐπὶ γῆς, instead of received Text, τῆς γῆς. The peculiar doxology is
repeated, as noted by Tischendorf on St. Matt.
vi. 13, by St. Gregory Nyssen, i. 1193, ἀπὸ τοῦ
πονηροῦ τοῦ ἐν τῷ κόσμῳ τούτῳ τὴν ἰσχὺν κεκτημένου,
οὗ ῥυσθείημεν χάριτι τοῦ Χριστοῦ, ὅτι αὐτῷ ἡ δύναμις
καὶ ἡ δόξα ἅμα τῷ Πατρὶ καὶ τῷ ἁγίῳ Πνεύματι, κ.τ.λ.

IX. 1. περὶ δὲ τῆς εὐχαριστίας. In this mention of the
Eucharist the cup is spoken of first, as in St.
Luke's Gospel. The prayers which follow can
hardly fail to strike the reader, as they differ so
much in tone and language from the rest of the
work. No doubt they are quoted from some unknown source, but it is noticeable that many of
the words and expressions are found in St. John's
Gospel alone.

2. τῆς ἁγίας ἀμπέλου. The holy vine of David seems
to be a mystical expression for our Lord. Bryennius quotes a passage from St. Clement of Alexandria, which seems to place this beyond doubt.
Quis dives salvus, § 29, οὗτος ὁ τὸν οἶνον τὸ αἷμα τῆς

ἀμπέλου τῆς Δαβὶδ ἐκχέας ἡμῶν ἐπὶ τὰς τετρωμένας ψυχάς. Migne, Gr. ix. 636. Another from the same writer is no less strong, τοῦτό μου ἐστιν τὸ αἶμα, αἶμα τῆς ἀμπέλου. Pædag. I., Migne, Gr. viii. 428. Comparing with these passages the fact that our Lord calls Himself "the Vine," and is spoken of by Isaiah (xl. 1) as a "branch out of the root of Jesse," it is hard to see why Harnack, who refers to these passages, should hesitate as to this interpretation. παιδός, 'child' or 'servant,' used, as in Acts iii. 13, 26; iv. 25 and 27, both of our Lord and of David. The use of the name Jesus, without the addition of Christ, is a mark of high antiquity.

3. εὐχαριστοῦμέν σοι. The view stated below, that we have here not the liturgical forms, strictly so-called, but rather some more popular or congregational prayers perhaps applicable to the agape, is corroborated by a passage in Ps. Athanasius, De Virginitate, § 13. Migne, Gr. iv. 266. The 'virgin' is directed ὅταν κατεσθίῃς ἐπὶ τῆς τραπέζης καὶ ἔρχῃ κλάσαι τὸν ἄρτον . . . εὐχαριστοῦσα λέγε, εὐχαριστοῦμέν σοι, Πάτερ ἡμῶν ὑπὲρ τῆς ἁγίας ἀναστάσεώς σου, διὰ γὰρ Ἰησοῦ τοῦ παιδός σου ἐγνώρισας ἡμῖν αὐτήν, καὶ καθὼς ὁ ἄρτος οὗτος διεσκορπισμένος ὑπῆρχεν ὁ ἐπάνω ταύτης τῆς τραπέζης καὶ συναχθεὶς ἐγένετο ἕν. οὕτως ἐπισυναχθήτω σου ἡ ἐκκλησία ἀπὸ τῶν περάτων τῆς γῆς εἰς τὴν βασιλείαν σου, ὅτι σου ἐστιν ἡ δύναμις καὶ ἡ δόξα εἰς τοὺς αἰῶνας· ἀμήν. καὶ ταύτην μὲν τὴν εὐχὴν ἐν τῷ κλᾷν τὸν ἄρτον καὶ θέλειν ἐσθίειν ὀφείλεις λέγειν. I am indebted for this reference to a notice of Dr. Swainson's Liturgies in the "Church Quarterly" for July. For the suggestion made

above, comp. Just. M. i. 67, ἀνιστάμεθα πάντες κοινῇ καὶ εὐχὰς πέμπομεν.

4. ἐπάνω τῶν ὀρέων. This phrase is peculiar in a work probably drawn up in Egypt; it corroborates the view that these prayers were not written by the author of the Διδαχή.

5. εὐχαριστίας applied to this sacrament. Cf. Just. Mart. Apol. i. 66, καὶ ἡ τροφὴ αὕτη καλεῖται παρ᾽ ἡμῶν εὐχαριστία, ἧς οὐδενὶ ἄλλῳ μετασχεῖν ἔξον ἐστὶν ἢ τῷ πιστεύοντι ἀληθῆ εἶναι τὰ δεδιδαγμένα ὑφ᾽ ἡμῶν καὶ λουσαμένῳ τὸ ὑπὲρ ἀφέσεως ἁμαρτιῶν καὶ εἰς ἀναγέννησιν λουτρὸν καὶ οὕτως βιοῦντι ὡς ὁ Χριστὸς παρέδωκεν.

X. 1. ἐμπλησθῆναι. Does the use of this expression, 'being filled,' refer to a full meal such as a love-feast, or, is it applied to communicating simply metaphorically? That the Apostolical Constitutions, vii. 26, 1, have changed it to μετὰ δὲ τὴν μετάληψιν, points rather to the former as the true interpretation. The love-feasts, though not always, yet so frequently accompanied the Eucharist, that it is difficult sometimes to say what is meant by *Cœna Domini*, the Lord's Supper. But the feasts seem, in the second century, to have been ordinarily held after communion, as Pliny says, in his often quoted letter to Trajan, 10. 96, "Quibus (the Eucharist) peractis morem sibi discedere, rursusque coëundi ad capiendum cibum." See Bingham, Eccl. Antiq. xv. vii. 6. If the Agape here preceded Communion, it speaks for the very high antiquity of the Διδαχή.

2. οὗ κατεσκήνωσας. This construction causes some

perplexity, as a transitive use of κατασκηνοῦν is
almost unsupported. One instance occurs in Ps.
xxii. 2, εἰς τόπον χλόης ἐκεῖ με κατεσκήνωσεν. Bryennius' explanation hardly satisfies: "that is,
which Thou didst write in our hearts, dwelling
in us," although, as he truly remarks, κατασκηνοῦν
τι ἔν τινι seems not to be found elsewhere. Harnack suggests that possibly ἐγνώρισας ἡμῖν has fallen
out before κατεσκήνωσας, and supports the suggestion by referring to John xvii. 26; but the Apost.
Const., vii. 26, also read οὗ κατεσκήνωσας.

3. ἐχαρίσω, not ἔδωκας, of spiritual gifts.

πνευματικὴν τροφὴν καὶ ποτὸν καὶ ζωὴν αἰώνιον.
Comp. Just. Mart. Apol. i. 66, οὐ γὰρ ὡς κοινὸν
ἄρτον οὐδὲ κοινὸν πόμα ταῦτα λαμβάνομεν; and, the
idea of the Eucharist being the "food of immortality," being somewhat more developed, Ignat.
ad Ephes. xx. ἕνα ἄρτον κλῶντες, ὅς ἐστιν φάρμακον
ἀθανασίας, ἀντίδοτος τοῦ μὴ ἀποθανεῖν, ἀλλὰ ζῆν ἐν
Ἰησοῦ Χριστῷ διὰ παντός. and comp. Iren. adv.
Hær. iv. 18. 3.

5. Harnack points out in this Eucharistic prayer
three divisions, and the different names by which
God is invoked in each. In the first, the εὐχαριστία, God is addressed as Holy Father, because
thanked for the gifts of revelation and eternal
life; in the second, the αἶνος καὶ δόξα, He is invoked as Almighty Ruler (δέσποτα), with reference to the work of Creation; and in the third
part, εὐχή, God is Κύριος, Lord over the Church.
The three divisions of the prayer are found in
Justin. Ap. i. 65.

σύναξον . . . ἁγιασθεῖσαν εἰς τὴν σὴν βασιλείαν.
Bryennius connects these last words, and under-
stands, "sanctified in order to inherit the kingdom
prepared for her." Harnack prefers inserting a
comma after ἁγιασθεῖσαν, and makes εἰς τὴν σὴν
βασιλείαν dependent upon σύναξον, as in ch. ix. 4.
The latter has been followed in the English translation, but with some hesitation. It is also
adopted by Duchesne in the *Bulletin Critique*,
1884, No. 5, p. 92.

6. St. Paul, 1 Cor. xi. 26, speaks of Christians as
shewing forth in the Holy Communion the Lord's
death, ἄχρις οὗ ἔλθῃ. Here the Death is passed
over, and the thought of the Coming again ex-
pands into a burst of prayer for the end. Bryennius contrasts Tertullian's statement, Apol. c. 39,
[Migne, i. 468,] "Oramus . . . pro mora finis."
The prayer in the Διδαχή agrees better with Rev.
xxii. 17, 20. Hilgenfeld, surely without ground,
thinks that these clauses savour of Montanism,
and suggests that the passage between the doxology and the Amen may have been interpolated.

ἐλθέτω χάρις. Cf. 1 Pet. i. 13, "the grace that is
to be brought unto you at the revelation of Jesus
Christ."

παρελθέτω ὁ κόσμος οὗτος. Cf. Rev. xxi. 1.

ὡσαννὰ τῷ Θεῷ Δαβίδ. This MS. reading is altered by Bryennius to υἱῷ, which is also adopted
by Hilgenfeld. But it is not easy to see any
reason for changing υἱῷ to Θεῷ (except the similarity of the letters), whilst the converse would
be very likely. Harnack points out that as Bar-

nabas Ep. xii. says. David would not call Christ his Son, but, φοβούμενος καὶ συνίων τὴν πλανὴν τῶν ἁμαρτωλῶν, called Him Lord, and there are other signs of a feeling in the second century against the title, Son of David. Probably, then, the MS. reading is the true one.

μαραναθά, i.e. "The Lord is coming," 1 Cor. xvi. 22. Here, according to liturgical analogy would be the place for Communion, if we have a form of Eucharistic service before us.

7. τοῖς δὲ προφήταις. There seems to have been a special freedom allowed to the prophets (cf. 1 Cor. xiv. 29, 31), as later on to the προεστώς. Just. M. Apol. i. 67. We must not, however, suppose that we have here a complete liturgy, or that such as yet existed. Rather the prayers here given are such as all might say, when no prophet was present, irrespective of any special liturgical prayers, containing the words of Institution and Lord's Prayer. Compare 1 Clem. xli., ἕκαστος ἡμῶν ἐν τῷ ἰδίῳ τάγματι εὐχαρεστείτω Θεῷ . . . μὴ παρεκβαίνων τὸν ὡρισμένον τῆς λειτουργίας αὐτοῦ κανόνα.

XI. 2. εἰς τὸ προσθεῖναι κ.τ.λ. Hilgenfeld again suspects Montanism here, and looks upon this as a recommendation of the false teachers of that sect.

3. περὶ δὲ τῶν ἀποστόλων καὶ προφητῶν. Amongst those, λαλοῦντες τὸν λόγον τοῦ Θεοῦ (iv. 1), are three different classes: first, the Apostles, whose duty it was to go from place to place, especially to open new fields of work. They are for some rea-

son kept under strict rule, and may never remain in one place. This would not have suited
St. Paul. Rules of this kind and those with
regard to prophets, which look as though perhaps the χαρίσματα were dying out, and worldly-
minded men making a profession for the sake of
gain, are the points which most weigh against
a very early date for the Διδαχή. But then in the
Epistles we find false teachers of various sorts.

Next Prophets (sometimes apparently the same
as Apostles; but note that in Acts xiii. 1, Barnabas and Saul are prophets and teachers before
being ordained to the Apostolate); and Teachers
(xiii. 1, 2; xv. 1, 2). These also travel, but are
permitted to settle, if they wish it, in any particular congregation, and then have a right to their
maintenance, (xiii. 3). ἡγούμενοι are mentioned
Heb. xiii. 7, as speakers of the word of God,
and in the first Epistle of St. Clement they are
often coupled with πρεσβύτεροι. As some writers
have laid stress on the omission of the latter class
in this passage, it may be well to refer to Tit. i.
5—7, which is unintelligible, unless the title
ἐπίσκοπος is equivalent to πρεσβύτερος, and may
refer in these early times to the same office.

Thirdly are mentioned (xv. 1, 2) Bishops and
Deacons, who are elected by the congregation, and
remain attached to it. As to the use of the title
Apostle, see Bp. Lightfoot, Galatians (Ed. iv.),
p. 92—101. The name Presbyter does not occur
in the Διδαχή, but (xv. 1, 2) we are told that the
bishops and deacons perform in their congrega-

tions the functions of the prophets and teachers,
(a bishop must, according to St. Paul, 1 Tim. iii. 2,
be "apt to teach," διδακτικός, cf. Tit. i. 9); and
of the prophets we are told again that they are
the 'high priests' of their people (xiii. 3). It is
impossible to discuss this question in a note, (Harnack has devoted an excursus of sixty-four pages,
besides notes, to the subject); but it may be fairly
asserted, that whilst the Διδαχή throws some light
upon the way in which the orders of the Christian
ministry were gradually assuming, at a particular
moment, their present functions, and whilst, as in
the New Testament, there was as yet no sharp
division with regard to some of the titles, it does
no more. Hilgenfeld, again, considers the passage
to refer to the apostles of Montanus.

4. πᾶς ἀπόστολος. The rules as to Apostles are
strict and simple. They are to be received "as
the Lord." They may stay nowhere beyond two
days, receive no money nor food more than enough
to take them to their next quarters. Eusebius,
H. E. v. 10, 2, [Migne, xx. 456,] calls them
Evangelists, ἦσαν γὰρ ἦσαν εἰσέτι τότε πλείους εὐαγ-
γελισταὶ τοῦ λόγου, ἔνθεον ζῆλον ἀποστολικοῦ μιμήματος
συνεισφέρειν ἐπ' αὐξήσει καὶ οἰκοδομῇ τοῦ θείου λόγου
προμηθούμενοι.

5. οὐ μενεῖ κ.τ.λ. There is something corrupt in the
text; perhaps Hilgenfeld's suggestion to omit οὐ
is the simplest alteration.

7. ἐν πνεύματι, in, i.e. under the influence of, the
Spirit. The prophetic utterance is thus spoken
of by Hermas. Pastor, Mand. xi. 8, 9, οὐδὲ ὅταν

θέλῃ ἄνθρωπος λαλεῖν, λαλεῖ τὸ πνεῦμα τὸ ἅγιον, ἀλλὰ τότε λαλεῖ ὅταν θελήσῃ αὐτὸ ὁ Θεὸς λαλεῖν. οὐ πειράσετε. Perhaps because all have not the gift of "discerning of spirits," 1 Cor. xii. 10, and so there would be danger of presumption. But see Rev. ii. 2. In outward behaviour and moral matters we find later on that a prophet may be judged.

8. τοὺς τρόπους Κυρίου. The test of true and false prophets is whether their manner and behaviour agree with those of Christ. Hermas, Past. Mand. xi. 8, says the same, and gives a list of qualities which mark a true prophet. Comp. St. Matt. vii. 16.

9. ὁρίζων τράπεζαν, "ordering a table," probably the holding of an Agape ordered in ecstasy. Possibly to guard against a false prophet doing this for his own benefit, followed by the subsequent warning.

11. ποιῶν εἰς μυστήριον κοσμικὸν κ.τ.λ. It seems hopeless to ascertain the meaning of this passage; several commentators and translators give different interpretations, and none are wholly satisfactory. Bryennius well suggests that it means some dramatic action from things in common life used to symbolize heavenly teaching, such as those performed by Isaiah, Jeremiah, Ezekiel, and Agabus. Evidently what was done was startling, perhaps suspicious, yet not necessarily evil, and so God alone could judge.

It might be understood, especially after the preceding passages, to have some reference to Sacraments, and teaching concerning them, could one trace this use of μυστήριον to a sufficiently early date, for ἐκκλησίας may be genitive.

Hilgenfeld and Harnack agree against Bryennius and Duchesne, in thinking that the "old prophets" mean Christian prophets of earlier date. Very possibly there is some corruption in the text, but as yet we have no clue to guide us in amending it. Hilgenfeld having assumed rather than proved the writer to be a Montanist, has altered and made the text capable of a Montanist interpretation. If his assumption be granted, his reading might be possible. Harnack, in a note very difficult to follow, endeavours to prove that the passage means abstaining from marriage.

XII. 1. πᾶς ἐρχόμενος. Every one professing to be a Christian is to be received, and his wants having been attended to, he is to be tested. But in no case may he remain permanently without working. Cf. 2 Thess. iii. 10—12.

σύνεσιν γὰρ ἕξετε. Bryennius suggests, in a letter to Harnack, that these words may be parenthetical, and this is the view taken in the translation, but perhaps σύνεσιν δεξιὰν καὶ ἀριστεράν, may mean "perfect understanding," comp. 2 Cor. vi. 7, ὅπλων τῆς δικαιοσύνης τῶν δεξιῶν καὶ ἀριστερῶν.

XIII. 1. πᾶς προφήτης . . . διδάσκαλος. If any genuine prophet or teacher wishes to settle in a congregation, he is to be maintained, and the first-fruits, with the limitation in v. 7, ὡς ἄν σοι δόξῃ, (the amount of first-fruits not being fixed by law,) are to be given to the prophets. Comp. Nehem. x. 37.

3. δώσεις in v. 4, δότε afterwards, again δός. The

singular is used of giving to the prophets as each one's duty. The poor, if there were no prophet to take charge of them, were the care of all.

4. ἐὰν δὲ μὴ κ.τ.λ. Were the poor not to be helped if there were a prophet? Is not the case rather that the prophet takes the place, when he is resident, afterwards assigned to the bishop, of seeing to the poor? The ἐπίσκοπος includes πρεσβύτερος, do some of these other offices not include the later ἐπίσκοπος?

XIV. 1. κυριακήν. The name given to the Lord's day, Rev. i. 10. The pleonasm caused by adding Κυρίου is strange but forcible. The noticeable feature is that the Eucharist is ordered as the special service for the Lord's day; the references to this in early Christian literature are numerous and well known, e.g. Just. Mart. Ap. i. 67. Apostolical Constitutions, ii. 59, 60.

προεξομολογησάμενοι. In chap. iv. confession in the Church was spoken of more generally. Here it is specially directed before the celebration of the Eucharist, and the reason given, "that your sacrifice may be pure." This is the only ancient direction for confession of sins as a public preliminary to the Eucharist; the clause does not appear in the corresponding section of the Apostolical Constitutions, vii. 30, but it explains some passages in other early writers.

2. ῥηθεῖσα ὑπὸ Κυρίου, [Mal. i. 11, 14]. This quotation does not agree verbally with the Septuagint, and omits, possibly on account of the heathen amongst whom these Christians were living, the

mention of incense. The passage is commonly
referred by early writers to the Eucharist (but
not to it alone), e.g. Just. M. Dial. 28, and elsewhere; Iren. iv. 17, 5; Tertull. adv. Jud. 5, &c.
Διδαχή, however, alone modifies the text.

XV. 1. Χειροτονήσατε. The selection of bishops and
deacons was, it seems, left to the congregation in
which they were to serve. Χειροτονεῖν is used,
Acts xiv. 23, of SS. Paul and Barnabas choosing
presbyters *for* the several congregations, and
2 Cor. viii. 19, of the selection made by the
churches of Titus to act with St. Paul in re-
ceiving the contributions made by the faithful.
Harnack looks upon these bishops and deacons
as specially the stewards, οἰκονόμοι, of the congregations, but we are told in this very passage that
they minister the same office as the prophets and
teachers, and are οἱ τετιμημένοι. See note on xi. 2,
and comp. Bingham, Chr. Ant. i. 46, ii. 15, &c.

πραεῖς καὶ ἀφιλαργύρους. Zahn suggests that these
officers, having to exercise discipline, are to be
meek, and as they have the care of the poor, must
not be fond of money.

2. οὖν. "Therefore." The mention of bishops and
deacons immediately upon that of the Eucharist
seems (against Harnack's view) to shew some
connection between them. Compare Clem. R.
1 Cor. xliv., τοὺς ἀμέμπτως καὶ ὁσίως προσενεγκόντας
τὰ δῶρα τῆς ἐπισκοπῆς ἀποβάλωμεν. And "bishops"
and deacons are constantly joined in speaking of
that service. Comp. for the third century the
well-known story of the martyrdom of St. Lau-

rence. The remarks of Bp. Lightfoot on Philip.
p. 191, tend to shew that the use of the term
bishop and not presbyter is a sign of writing to
Gentiles rather than Jews.

3. Comp. Matt. xviii. 15—17. The sense is fairly
clear, that every kind of private quarrel or dis-
agreement is to be absolutely put down. The
construction, ἀστοχεῖν κατά τινος, does not seem to
occur elsewhere.

I should prefer Hilgenfeld's reading ἀκουέσθω,
and translate, Let no one speak nor listen to
him.

XVI. Hilgenfeld again insists that almost the whole
of this chapter is a Montanistic addition, but
although it may be true that some phrases might
have been written by a Montanist, there is no
convincing proof. "The end" was always in the
thoughts of the early Christians, even if the writer
of this treatise does not expect it so immediately
as some others. The passage may be compared
with Matt. xxiv. 42—44; Luke xii. 35; 2 Tim.
iii. 1—7; and 2 Pet. iii.

1. οἱ λύχνοι κ.τ.λ. The text here is neither wholly
St. Matthew nor St. Luke, and again, as in I. 4,
Tatian's Diatessaron supports the mixed text.

2. συναχθήσεσθε. Comp. Heb. x. 24, 25. The necessity of final perseverance insisted upon, and, as
leading towards it, constant meeting together in
prayer. Comp. Barn. Ep. ch. iv. διὸ προσέχωμεν
ἐν ἐσχάταις ἡμέραις· οὐδὲν γὰρ ὠφελήσει ὁ πᾶς χρόνος
τῆς ζωῆς ἡμῶν καὶ τῆς πίστεως ἐὰν μὴ νῦν ἐν τῷ ἀνόμῳ
καιρῷ ἀντιστῶμεν. and Ezek. xxxiii. 13.

ἀνήκοντα. Cf. Clem. R. 1 Cor. xlv. ἐστέ . . . .
ζηλωταὶ περὶ τῶν ἀνηκόντων εἰς σωτηρίαν.

3. ἐν ἐσχάταις ἡμέραις. Comp. 2 Pet. iii. 3; Matt.
xxiv. 10—13.

5. ὑπ᾽ αὐτοῦ τοῦ καταθέματος. Bryennius, followed by
Harnack, accepts the MS. reading ὑπό, and thinks
that by κατάθεμα (= κατανάθεμα) may be meant
Christ, whom those who are "offended" will curse.
He also suggests as a reading, ἐπ᾽ αὐτοῦ τοῦ κάτω
θέματος, i.e. the earth, but Harnack rightly remarks that αὐτοῦ is against this reading. Hilgenfeld's suggestion, ἀπό, goes far to remove all
difficulties. The word κατάθεμα is adopted by
the N. T. revisers in Rev. xxii. 3. Bryennius,
in a letter to Harnack, quoted by the latter *ad loc.*,
makes a later suggestion that κατάθεμα may mean
the being joined with those who are offended and
perish; or, the world deceiver himself; or, the
curse of God generally, from which those who
are then faithful will be wholly delivered for
ever. The latter seems the most satisfactory.

6. σημεῖα. These signs seem to agree with Matt.
xxiv. 30, 31. 1. The sign of the Son of Man
seen in the opening heaven, what the special
"sign" may be the writer does not say; 2. The
sound of the trumpet; 3. The gathering together
of the elect. For it is to be noted that the resurrection is specially limited in v. 7. Probably the
passages, 1 Thess. iv. 16, 17, 1 Cor. xv. 52, were
not known to the writer of the Διδαχή, but the
teaching is the same, and the difficulty some have
found in reconciling these passages with the

Διδαχή may be solved by remarking, (1) that the latter does not speak of those who are alive, and (2) that the coming of the Lord, the voice of the angel, and the resurrection will all take place "in a moment, in the twinkling of an eye," and so be to human senses simultaneous; the end being as in this work, "Then shall the world see the Lord coming upon the clouds of heaven."

These last lines speaking of the resurrection, "but not of all," coupled with the quotation from Zechariah, *may* denote a tendency to Montanism, as Millenarianism was strongly held by that party. But Christ Himself says that the angels will be sent to "gather together the *elect*," Matt. xxiv. 31. Cp. 1 Cor. xv. 23; Rev. xx. 4, 5.

INDEX

OF THE MORE NOTICEABLE WORDS AND PHRASES
WHICH OCCUR IN THE Διδαχή.

Uniform with the present Work.

De Fide et Symbolo:

Documenta Quædam nec non Aliquorum SS. Patrum Tractatus. Edidit CAROLUS A. HEURTLEY, S.T.P., Dom. Margaretæ Prælector, et Ædis Christi Canonicus. Editio Tertia, Recognita et Aucta. Crown 8vo., cloth, 4s. 6d.

S. Athanasius on the Incarnation, &c.

S. Patris Nostri S. Athanasii Archiepiscopi Alexandriæ de Incarnatione Verbi, ejusque Corporali ad nos Adventu. With an English Translation by the Rev. J. RIDGWAY, B.D., Hon. Canon of Ch. Ch. Fcap. 8vo., cloth, 5s.

The Canons of the Church.

The Definitions of the Catholic Faith and Canons of Discipline of the First Four General Councils of the Universal Church. In Greek and English. Fcap. 8vo., cloth, 2s. 6d.

The English Canons.

The Constitutions and Canons Ecclesiastical of the Church of England, referred to their Original Sources, and Illustrated with Explanatory Notes, by MACKENZIE E. C. WALCOTT, B.D., F.S.A., Præcentor and Prebendary of Chichester. Fcap. 8vo., cloth, 2s. 6d.

The Athanasian Creed.

A Critical History of the Athanasian Creed, by the Rev. DANIEL WATERLAND, D.D. Fcap. 8vo., cloth, 5s.

S. Aurelius Augustinus,

EPISCOPUS HIPPONENSIS,

De Catechizandis Rudibus, de Fide Rerum quæ non videntur, de Utilitate Credendi. In Usum Juniorum. Edidit C. MARRIOTT, S.T.B., olim Coll. Oriel. Socius. A New Edition. Fcap. 8vo., cloth, 3s. 6d.

The Pastoral Rule of S. Gregory.

Sancti Gregorii Papæ Regulæ Pastoralis Liber, ad JOHANNEM, Episcopum Civitatis Ravennæ. With an English Translation. By the Rev. H. R. BRAMLEY, M.A., Fellow of Magdalen College, Oxford. Fcap. 8vo., cloth, 6s.

OXFORD AND LONDON: PARKER AND CO.

A SELECTION FROM THE PUBLICATIONS OF
PARKER AND CO.

OXFORD, AND 6 SOUTHAMPTON-STREET,
STRAND, LONDON.

A Historical Companion to Hymns Ancient and Modern;

Containing the Greek and Latin; the German, Italian, French,
Danish and Welsh Hymns; the first lines of the English
Hymns; the Names of all Authors and Translators; Notes
and Dates. Edited by the Rev. ROBERT MAUDE MOORSOM,
M.A., Trin. Coll., Cambridge, formerly Rector of Sadberge,
County Durham. 24mo., cloth, 5s.

The Apology of Tertullian for the Christians.

Translated with Introduction, Analysis, and Appendix containing the Letters of Pliny and Trajan respecting the Christians. By T. HERBERT BINDLEY, M.A., Merton College,
Oxford. Crown 8vo., cloth, 3s. 6d.

A Short History of Clent.

By JOHN AMPHLETT, M.A., S.C.L., Barrister-at-Law. Crown
8vo., cloth, 5s.

A Brief History of the English Church.

By ALFRED CECIL SMITH, M.A., Vicar of Summertown,
Oxford. Fcap. 8vo., limp cloth, price 2s. 6d.

The Faithful Departed

And Other SERMONS. By the Rev. CHARLES PAGE EDEN,
M.A., sometime Fellow and Tutor of Oriel College, and
Vicar of St. Mary's, Oxford; late Vicar of Aberford, and
Canon of York. Crown 8vo., cloth, 5s.

A Menology;

Or Record of Departed Friends. 16mo., cloth, 3s.

The Seven Sayings from the Cross:

ADDRESSES by WILLIAM BRIGHT, D.D., Canon of Christ
Church, Oxford. Fcap. 8vo., limp cloth, 1s. 6d.

Lays of the Early English Church.

By W. FOXLEY NORRIS, M.A., Rector of Witney. Fcap. 8vo.,
cloth, with Twelve Illustrations, 3s. 6d.

Lost Chords.

By W. MOORE, Rector of Appleton; late Fellow of Magdalen
College, Oxford. Fcap. 8vo., cloth, 3s.

The Church in England from William III. to Victoria.

By the Rev. A. H. HORE, M.A., Trinity College, Oxford.
2 vols., Post 8vo., cloth, 15s.

[290.1.2m.]

The One Religion.

Truth, Holiness, and Peace desired by the Nations, and Revealed by Jesus Christ. By the Right Rev. the LORD BISHOP OF SALISBURY. Second Edition. Crown 8vo., cloth, 7s. 6d.

The Administration of the Holy Spirit .

IN THE BODY OF CHRIST. The Bampton Lectures for 1868. By the late LORD BISHOP OF SALISBURY. Third Edition. Crown 8vo., 7s. 6d.

An Explanation of the Thirty-Nine Articles.

By the late A. P. FORBES, D.C.L., Bishop of Brechin. With an Epistle Dedicatory to the Rev. E. B. PUSEY, D.D. New Edition, in one vol., Post 8vo., 12s.

A Short Explanation of the Nicene Creed,

For the Use of Persons beginning the Study of Theology. By the late A. P. FORBES, D.C.L., Bishop of Brechin. New Edition, Crown 8vo., cloth, 6s.

The Apostles' Creed.

The Greek Origin of the Apostles' Creed Illustrated by Ancient Documents and Recent Research. By Rev. JOHN BARON, D.D., F.S.A. 8vo., cloth, with Seven Illustrations, 10s. 6d.

The Sacraments.

RICHARD BAXTER ON THE SACRAMENTS: Holy Orders, Holy Baptism, Confirmation, Absolution, Holy Communion. 18mo., cloth, 1s.

The History of Confirmation.

By WILLIAM JACKSON, M.A., Queen's College, Oxford; Vicar of Heathfield, Sussex. Crown 8vo., cloth, 2s. 6d.

A Summary of the Ecclesiastical Courts Commission's Report:

And of Dr. STUBBS' Historical Reports; together with a Review of the Evidence before the Commission. By SPENCER L. HOLLAND, Barrister-at-Law. Post 8vo., cloth, 7s. 6d.

A History of Canon Law

In conjunction with other Branches of Jurisprudence: with Chapters on the Royal Supremacy and the Report of the Commission on Ecclesiastical Courts. By Rev. J. DODD, M.A., formerly Rector of Hampton Poyle, Oxon. 8vo., cloth, 7s. 6d.

The Philosophy of Church-Life,

Or The Church of Christ viewed as the Means whereby God manifests Himself to Mankind. By the late R. TUDOR, B.A., Vicar of Swallowcliffe, Wilts; Author of "The Decalogue viewed as the Christian's Law," &c. 2 vols., 8vo., cloth, 16s.

"A work which we do not hesitate to pronounce one of the most important contributions to scientific theology that has been made in our time."—*John Bull.*

On Eucharistical Adoration.

With Considerations suggested by a Pastoral Letter on the Doctrine of the Most Holy Eucharist. By the late Rev. JOHN KEBLE, M.A., Vicar of Hursley. 24mo., sewed, 2s.

The Catholic Doctrine of the Sacrifice and Participation of the Holy Eucharist.

By GEORGE TREVOR, M.A., D.D., Canon of York; Rector of Beeford. Second Edition. 8vo., cloth, 10s. 6d.

S. Athanasius on the Incarnation, &c.

S. Patris Nostri S. Athanasii Archiepiscopi Alexandriæ de Incarnatione Verbi, ejusque Corporali ad nos Adventu. With an English Translation by the Rev. J. RIDGWAY, B.D., Hon. Canon of Ch. Ch. Fcap. 8vo., cloth, 5s.

De Fide et Symbolo:

Documenta quædam nec non Aliquorum SS. Patrum Tractatus. Edidit CAROLUS A. HEURTLEY, S.T.P., Dom. Margaretæ Prælector, et Ædis Christi Canonicus. Editio Quarta, Recognita et Aucta. Crown 8vo., cloth, 4s. 6d.

Translation of the above.
Cloth, 4s. 6d.

The Canons of the Church.

The Definitions of the Catholic Faith and Canons of Discipline of the First Four General Councils of the Universal Church. In Greek and English. Fcap. 8vo., cloth, 2s. 6d.

The English Canons.

The Constitutions and Canons Ecclesiastical of the Church of England, referred to their Original Sources, and Illustrated with Explanatory Notes, by MACKENZIE E. C. WALCOTT, B.D., F.S.A., Præcentor and Prebendary of Chichester. Fcap. 8vo., cloth, 2s. 6d.

Our Deus Homo.

Or Why God was made Man; by ST. ANSELM. Latin and English.

St. Cyril on the Mysteries.

The Five Lectures of St. Cyril on the Mysteries, and other Sacramental Treatises; with Translations. Edited by the Rev. H. DE ROMESTIN, M.A., Great Maplestead, Essex. Fcap. 8vo., cloth. 3s.

S. Aurelius Augustinus,
EPISCOPUS HIPPONENSIS,

De Catechizandis Rudibus, de Fide Rerum quæ non videntur, de Utilitate Credendi. A New Edition with the Enchiridion. Fcap. 8vo., cloth, 3s. 6d.

Translation of the above.
Cloth, 3s. 6d.

Vincentius Lirinensis.

For the Antiquity and Universality of the Catholic Faith against the Profane Novelties of all Heretics. *Latin and English.* New Edition, Fcap. 8vo., 3s.

The Pastoral Rule of S. Gregory.

Sancti Gregorii Papæ Regulæ Pastoralis Liber, ad JOHANNEM, Episcopum Civitatis Ravennæ. With an English Translation. By the Rev. H. R. BRAMLEY, M.A., Fellow of Magdalen College, Oxford. Fcap. 8vo., cloth, 6s.

The Book of Ratramn.

The Priest and Monk of Corbey commonly called Bertram, on the Body and Blood of the Lord. (Latin and English.) Fcap. 8vo.

The Athanasian Creed.

A Critical History of the Athanasian Creed, by the Rev. DANIEL WATERLAND, D.D. Fcap. 8vo., cloth, 5s.

Διδαχὴ τῶν δώδεκα Ἀποστόλων.

The Teaching of the Twelve Apostles. The Greek Text with English Translation, Introduction, Notes, and Illustrative Passages. By the Rev. H. DE ROMESTIN, Incumbent of Freeland, and Rural Dean. Second Edition. Fcap. 8vo., cloth, 3s.

Studia Sacra:

Commentaries on the Introductory Verses of St. John's Gospel, and on a Portion of St. Paul's Epistle to the Romans; with an Analysis of St. Paul's Epistles, &c., by the late Rev. JOHN KEBLE, M.A. 8vo., cloth, 10s. 6d.

Discourses on Prophecy.

In which are considered its Structure, Use and Inspiration. By JOHN DAVISON, B.D. Sixth and Cheaper Edition. 8vo., cloth, 9s.

The Worship of the Old Covenant

CONSIDERED MORE ESPECIALLY IN RELATION TO THAT OF THE New. By the Rev. E. F. WILLIS, M.A., late Vice-Principal of Cuddesdon College. Post 8vo., cloth, 5s.

A Summary of the Evidences for the Bible.

By the Rev. T. S. ACKLAND, M.A., late Fellow of Clare Hall, Cambridge ; Incumbent of Pollington cum Balne, Yorkshire. 24mo., cloth, 3s.

A Plain Commentary on the Book of Psalms

(Prayer-book Version), chiefly grounded on the Fathers. For the Use of Families. 2 vols., Fcap. 8vo., cloth, 10s. 6d.

The Psalter and the Gospel.

The Life, Sufferings, and Triumph of our Blessed Lord, revealed in the Book of Psalms. Fcap. 8vo., cloth, 2s.

The Study of the New Testament:

Its Present Position, and some of its Problems. AN INAU-GURAL LECTURE delivered on Feb. 20th and 22nd, 1883. By W. SANDAY, M.A., D.D., Dean Ireland's Professor of the Exegesis of Holy Scripture. 64 pp. 8vo., in wrapper, 2s.

Sayings Ascribed to Our Lord

By the Fathers and other Primitive Writers, and Incidents in His Life narrated by them, otherwise than found in Scripture. By JOHN THEODORE DODD, B.A., late Student of Christ Church, Oxford. Fcap. 8vo., cloth, 3s.

A Commentary on the Epistles and Gospels in the Book of Common Prayer.

Extracted from Writings of the Fathers of the Holy Catholic Church, anterior to the Division of the East and West. With an Introductory Notice by the DEAN OF ST. PAUL'S. 2 vols., Crown 8vo., cloth, 10s. 6d.

Catena Aurea.

A Commentary on the Four Gospels, collected out of the Works
of the Fathers by S. THOMAS AQUINAS. Uniform with the
Library of the Fathers. A Re-issue, complete in 6 vols.,
cloth, £2 2s.

A Plain Commentary on the Four Holy Gospels,

Intended chiefly for Devotional Reading. By the Very Rev.
J. W. BURGON, B.D., Dean of Chichester. New Edition.
. 4 vols., Fcap. 8vo., limp cloth, £1 1s.

The Last Twelve Verses of the Gospel according to S. Mark

Vindicated against Recent Critical Objectors and Established,
by the Very Rev. J. W. BURGON, B.D., Dean of Chichester.
With Facsimiles of Codex ℵ and Codex L. 8vo., cloth, 6s.

The Gospels from a Rabbinical Point of View,

Shewing the perfect Harmony of the Four Evangelists on the
subject of our Lord's Last Supper, and the Bearing of the
Laws and Customs of the Jews at the time of our Lord's
coming on the Language of the Gospels. By the late Rev. G.
W. PIERITZ, M.A. Crown 8vo., limp cloth, 3s.

Christianity as Taught by S. Paul.

By the late W. J. IRONS, D.D., of Queen's College, Oxford;
Prebendary of S. Paul's; being the BAMPTON LECTURES
for the Year 1870, with an Appendix of the CONTINUOUS
SENSE of S. Paul's Epistles; with Notes and Metalegomena,
8vo., with Map, Second Edition, with New Preface, cloth, 9s.

S. Paul's Epistles to the Ephesians and Philippians.

A Practical and Exegetical Commentary. Edited by the late
Rev. HENRY NEWLAND. 8vo., cloth, 7s. 6d.

The Explanation of the Apocalypse.

By VENERABLE BEDA, Translated by the Rev. EDW. MAR-
SHALL, M.A., F.S.A., formerly Fellow of Corpus Christi
College, Oxford. 180 pp. Fcap. 8vo., cloth, 3s. 6d.

A History of the Church,

From the Edict of Milan, A.D. 313, to the Council of Chalcedon, A.D. 451. By WILLIAM BRIGHT, D.D., Regius Professor of Ecclesiastical History, and Canon of Christ Church, Oxford. Second Edition. Post 8vo., 10s. 6d.

The Age of the Martyrs;

Or, The First Three Centuries of the Work of the Church of our Lord and Saviour Jesus Christ. By the late JOHN DAVID JENKINS, B.D., Fellow of Jesus College, Oxford; Canon of Pieter Maritzburg. Cr. 8vo., cl., reduced to 3s. 6d.

The Church in England from William III. to Victoria.

By the Rev. A. H. HORE, M.A., Trinity College, Oxford. 2 vols., Post 8vo., cloth, 15s.

The Ecclesiastical History of the First Three Centuries,

From the Crucifixion of Jesus Christ to the year 313. By the late Rev. Dr. BURTON. Fourth Edition. 8vo., cloth, 12s.

A Brief History of the Christian Church,

From the First Century to the Reformation. By the Rev. J. S. BARTLETT. Fcap. 8vo., cloth, 2s. 6d.

A History of the English Church,

From its Foundation to the Reign of Queen Mary. By MARY CHARLOTTE STAPLEY. Fourth Edition, revised, with a Re-commendatory Notice by DEAN HOOK. Crown 8vo., cloth, 5s.

Bede's Ecclesiastical History of the English Nation.

A New Translation by the Rev. L. GIDLEY, M.A., Chaplain of St. Nicholas', Salisbury. Crown 8vo., cloth, 6s.

St. Paul in Britain;

Or, The Origin of British as opposed to Papal Christianity. By the Rev. R. W. MORGAN. Second Edition. Crown 8vo., cloth, 2s. 6d.

The Sufferings of the Clergy during the Great Rebellion.

By the Rev. JOHN WALKER, M.A., sometime of Exeter College, Oxford, and Rector of St. Mary Major, Exeter. Epitomised by the Author of "The Annals of England." Second Edition. Fcap. 8vo.. cloth, 2s. 6d.

Missale ad usum Insignis et Præclaræ Ecclesiæ Sarum.

Ed. F. H. DICKINSON, A.M. Complete in One Vol., 8vo., cl., 26s. Part II., 6s.; Part III., 10s. 6d.; and Part IV., 7s. 6d.; may still be had.

The First Prayer-Book of Edward VI. Compared

With the Successive Revisions of the Book of Common Prayer. Together with a Concordance and Index to the Rubrics in the several Editions. Second Edition. Crown 8vo., cloth, 12s.

An Introduction

TO THE HISTORY OF THE SUCCESSIVE REVI-sions of the Book of Common Prayer. By JAMES PARKER, Hon. M.A. Oxon. Crown 8vo., pp. xxxii., 532, cloth, 12s.

The Principles of Divine Service;

Or, An Inquiry concerning the True Manner of Understand-ing and Using the Order for Morning and Evening Prayer, and for the Administration of the Holy Communion in the English Church. By the late Ven. PHILIP FREEMAN, M.A., Archdeacon of Exeter, &c. 2 vols., 8vo., cloth, 16s.

A History of the Book of Common Prayer,

And other Authorized Books, from the Reformation; with an Account of the State of Religion in England from 1640 to 1660. By the Rev. THOMAS LATHBURY, M.A. Second Edition, with an Index. 8vo., cloth, 5s.

The Prayer-Book Calendar.

THE CALENDAR OF THE PRAYER-BOOK ILLUS-TRATED. (Comprising the first portion of the "Calendar of the Anglican Church," with additional Illustrations, an Appendix on Emblems, &c.) With 200 Engravings from Me-dieval Works of Art. Sixth Thousand. Fcap. 8vo., cl., 6s.

A CHEAP EDITION OF

The First Prayer-Book

As issued by the Authority of the Parl'ament of the Second Year of King Edward VI. 1549. Tenth Thousand. 24mo., limp cloth, price 1s.

Also,

The Second Prayer-Book of Edward VI.

Issued 1552. Fifth Thousand. 24mo., limp cloth, price 1s.

Ritual Conformity.

Interpretations of the Rubrics of the Prayer-Book, agreed upon by a Conference held at All Saints, Margaret-street, 1880—1881. Third Edition, 80 pp. Crown 8vo., in wrapper, 1s.

The Ornaments Rubrick,

ITS HISTORY AND MEANING. Fifth Thousand. 72 pp., Crown 8vo., 6d.

The Catechist's Manual;

By EDW. M. HOLMES, Rector of Marsh Gibbon, Bicester. With an Introduction by the late SAMUEL WILLERFORCE, LORD BP. OF WINCHESTER. 6th Thousand. Cr. 8vo., limp cl., 5s.

The Confirmation Class-book:

Notes for Lessons, with APPENDIX, containing Questions and Summaries for the Use of the Candidates. By EDWARD M. HOLMES, LL.B., Author of the "Catechist's Manual." Second Edition, Fcap. 8vo., limp cloth, 2s. 6d.

THE QUESTIONS, separate, 4 sets, in wrapper, 1s.
THE SUMMARIES, separate, 4 sets, in wrapper, 1s.

Catechetical Lessons on the Book of Common Prayer.

Illustrating the Prayer-book, from its Title-page to the end of the Collects, Epistles, and Gospels. Designed to aid the Clergy in Public Catechising. By the Rev. Dr. FRANCIS HESSEY, Incumbent of St. Barnabas, Kensington. Fcap. 8vo., cloth, 6s.

Catechising Notes on the Apostles' Creed;

The Ten Commandments; The Lord's Prayer; The Confirmation Service; The Forms of Prayer at Sea, &c. By A WORCESTERSHIRE CURATE. Crown 8vo., in wrapper, 1s.

The Church's Work in our Large Towns.

By GEORGE HUNTINGTON, M.A., Rector of Tenby, and Domestic Chaplain of the Rt. Hon. the Earl of Crawford and Balcarres. Second Edit., revised and enlarged. Cr. 8vo., cl. 3s. 6d.

Notes of Seven Years' Work in a Country Parish.

By R. F. WILSON, M.A., Prebendary of Sarum, and Examining Chaplain to the Bishop of Salisbury. Fcap. 8vo., cloth, 4s.

A Manual of Pastoral Visitation,

Intended for the Use of the Clergy in their Visitation of the Sick and Afflicted. By A PARISH PRIEST. Dedicated, by permission, to His Grace the Archbishop of Dublin. Second Edition, Crown 8vo., limp cloth, 3s. 6d. ; roan, 4s.

The Cure of Souls.

By the Rev. G. ARDEN, M.A., Rector of Winterborne-Came, and Author of "Breviates from Holy Scripture," &c. Fcap. 8vo., cloth, 2s. 6d.

Questions on the Collects, Epistles, and Gospels,

Throughout the Year. Edited by the Rev. T. L. CLAUGHTON, Vicar of Kidderminster. For the Use of Teachers in Sunday Schools. Fifth Edition, 18mo., cl. In two Parts, *each* 2s. 6d.

Addresses to the Candidates for Ordination on the Questions in the Ordination Service.

By the late SAMUEL WILBERFORCE, LORD BISHOP OF WINCHESTER. Fifth Thousand. Crown 8vo., cloth, 6s.

Tracts for the Christian Seasons.

FIRST SERIES. Edited by JOHN ARMSTRONG, D.D., late
Lord Bishop of Grahamstown. 4 vols. complete, Fcap. 8vo.,
cloth, 12s.

SECOND SERIES. Edited by JOHN ARMSTRONG, D.D., late
Lord Bishop of Grahamstown. 4 vols. complete, Fcap. 8vo.,
cloth, 10s.

THIRD SERIES. Edited by JAMES RUSSELL WOODFORD, D.D.,
late Lord Bishop of Ely. 4 vols., Fcap. 8vo., cloth, 14s.

Faber's Stories from the Old Testament.

With Four Illustrations. New Edition. Square Crown 8vo.,
cloth, 4s.

Holy Order.

A CATECHISM. By CHARLES S. GRUEBER, Vicar of
S. James, Hambridge, Diocese of Bath and Wells. 220 pp.
24mo., in wrapper, 3s.

By the same Author.

The Church of England the Ancient Church of the Land.

Its Property. Disestablishment and Disendowment. Fate of
Sacrilege. Work and Progress of the Church, &c., &c.
A CATECHISM. Second Edition, 24mo., in wrapper, 1s.

A Catechism on the Kingdom of God :

For the Use of the Children of the Kingdom in Sunday and
Day Schools. Second Edition, 70 pp. 24mo., cloth, 1s.; in
stiff wrapper, 6d.

" Is Christ Divided ? "

On Unity in Religion, and the Sin and Scandal of Schism,
That is to say, of Division, Disunion, Separation, among
Christians. A CATECHISM. 8vo., in wrapper, 1s.

The Catechism of the Church of England

Commented upon, and Illustrated from the Holy Scriptures
and the Book of Common Prayer, with Appendices on Confirmation, &c., &c. 24mo., limp cloth, 1s.; cloth boards,
1s. 6d.

For a Series of Parochial Books and Tracts published by
Messrs. Parker, see the Parochial Catalogue.

Oxford Editions of Devotional Works.

*Fcap. 8vo., chiefly printed in Red and Black, on Toned Paper.
Also kept in a variety of Leather Bindings.*

Andrewes' Devotions.
DEVOTIONS. By the Right Rev.
LANCELOT ANDREWES. Trans-
lated from the Greek and Latin,
and arranged anew. Cloth, 5*s.*

The Imitation of Christ.
FOUR BOOKS. By THOMAS A
KEMPIS. A new Edition, re-
vised. Cloth, 4*s.*
Pocket Edition. 32mo., cloth, 1*s.* ;
bound, 1*s. 6d.*

Laud's Devotions.
THE PRIVATE DEVOTIONS of
Dr. WILLIAM LAUD, Archbishop
of Canterbury, and Martyr. Antique cloth, 5*s.*

Spinckes' Devotions.
TRUE CHURCH OF ENGLAND
MAN'S COMPANION IN THE
CLOSET. By NATHANIEL
SPINCKES. Floriated borders,
antique cloth, 4*s.*

Sutton's Meditations.
GODLY MEDITATIONS UPON
THE MOST HOLY SACRA-
MENT OF THE LORD'S
SUPPER. By CHRISTOPHER
SUTTON, D.D., late Prebend of
Westminster. A new Edition.
Antique cloth, 5*s.*

Devout Communicant.
THE DEVOUT COMMUNI-
CANT, exemplified in his Be-
haviour before, at, and after the
Sacrament of the Lord's Supper :
Practically suited to all the Parts
of that Solemn Ordinance. 7th
Edition, revised. Edited by Rev.
G. MOULTRIE. Fcap. 8vo., toned
paper, red lines, ant. cloth, 4*s.*

Taylor's Holy Living.
THE RULE AND EXERCISES
OF HOLY LIVING. By BI-
SHOP JEREMY TAYLOR. Antique
cloth, 4*s.*
Pocket Edition. 32mo., cloth, 1*s.* ;
bound, 1*s. 6d.*

Taylor's Holy Dying.
THE RULE AND EXERCISES
OF HOLY DYING. By BISHOP
JEREMY TAYLOR. Ant. cloth, 4*s.*
Pocket Edition. 32mo., cloth, 1*s.*
bound, 1*s. 6d.*

Taylor's Golden Grove.
THE GOLDEN GROVE : A
Choice Manual, containing what
is to be Believed, Practised, and
Desired or Prayed for. By BI-
SHOP JEREMY TAYLOR. Antique
cloth, 3*s. 6d.*

Wilson's Sacra Privata.
SACRA PRIVATA. The Private
Meditations, Devotions, and Pray-
ers of the Right Rev. T. WILSON,
D.D., Lord Bishop of Sodor and
Man. Now first Printed entire,
from the Original Manuscripts.
Antique cloth, 4*s.*

ΕΙΚΩΝ ΒΑΣΙΛΙΚΗ.
THE PORTRAITURE OF HIS
SACRED MAJESTY KING
CHARLES I. in his Solitudes
and Sufferings. New Edition,
with an Historical Preface by
C. M. PHILLIMORE. Cloth, 5*s.*

Ancient Collects.
ANCIENT COLLECTS AND
OTHER PRAYERS, Selected
for Devotional Use from various
Rituals, with an Appendix on the
Collects in the Prayer-book. By
WILLIAM BRIGHT, D.D. Fourth
Edition. Antique cloth, 5*s.*

EUCHARISTICA:

Meditations and Prayers on the Most Holy Eucharist, from Old English Divines. With an Introduction by SAMUEL, LORD BISHOP OF OXFORD. A New Edition, revised by the Rev. H. E. CLAYTON, Vicar of S. Mary Magdalene, Oxford. In Red and Black, 32mo., cloth, 2s. 6d.—Cheap Edition, 1s.

DAILY STEPS TOWARDS HEAVEN ;

Or, PRACTICAL THOUGHTS on the GOSPEL HISTORY, for Every Day in the Year. Fiftieth Thousand. 32mo., roan, 2s. 6d. ; morocco, 5s.

LARGE-TYPE EDITION. Crown 8vo., cloth antique, 5s.

THE HOURS:

Being Prayers for the Third, Sixth, and Ninth Hours; with a Preface and Heads of Devotion for the Day. Seventh Edition. 32mo., 1s.

PRIVATE PRAYERS FOR A WEEK.

Compiled by WILLIAM BRIGHT, D.D., Canon of Christ Church, Oxford. 96 pp. Fcap. 8vo., limp cloth, 1s. 6d.

By the same Author.

FAMILY PRAYERS FOR A WEEK.

Fcap. 8vo., cloth, 1s.

STRAY THOUGHTS:

For Every Day in the Year. Collected and Arranged by E. L. 32mo., cloth gilt, red edges, 1s.

OUTLINES OF INSTRUCTIONS

Or Meditations for the Church's Seasons. By the late JOHN KEBLE, M.A. Edited, with a Preface, by the late R. F. WILSON, M.A. Second Edition. Crown 8vo., cloth, toned paper, 5s.

SPIRITUAL COUNSEL, ETC.

By the late Rev. J. KEBLE, M.A. Edited by the late R. F. WILSON, M.A. Fifth Edition. Post 8vo., cloth, 3s. 6d.

MEDITATIONS FOR THE FORTY DAYS OF LENT.

By the Author of "Charles Lowder." With a Prefatory Notice by the ARCHBISHOP OF DUBLIN. 18mo., cloth, 2s. 6d.

OF THE IMITATION OF CHRIST.

Four Books. By THOMAS A KEMPIS. Small 4to., printed on thick toned paper, with red border-lines, &c. Cloth, 12s.

PRAYERS FOR MARRIED PERSONS.

From Various Sources, chiefly from the Ancient Liturgies. Se-lected by C. WARD, M.A. Third Edition, Revised. 24mo., cloth, 4s. 6d. ; Cheap Edition, 2s. 6d.

FOR THE LORD'S SUPPER.

DEVOTIONS BEFORE AND AFTER HOLY COMMUNION. With Preface by J. KEBLE. Sixth Edition. 32mo., cloth, 2s. With the Office, cloth, 2s. 6d.

The late Osborne Gordon.

OSBORNE GORDON. A Memoir : with a Selection of his Writings. Edited by Geo. Marshall, M.A., Rector of Milton, Berks, &c. With Medallion Portrait, 8vo., cloth, 10s. 6d.

Dr. Preston.

THE LIFE OF THE RENOWNED DR. PRESTON. Writ by his Pupil, Master Thomas Ball, D.D., Minister of Northampton in the year 1628. Edited by E. W. Harcourt, Esq., M.P. Crown 8vo., cloth, 4s.

Rev. John Keble.

A MEMOIR OF THE REV. JOHN KEBLE, M.A., late Vicar of Hursley. By the Right Hon. Sir J. T. Coleridge, D.C.L. Fifth Edition. Post 8vo., cloth, 6s.

OCCASIONAL PAPERS AND REVIEWS, on Sir Walter Scott, Poetry, and Sacred Poetry. By the late Rev. John Keble. Author of "The Christian Year." Demy 8vo., cloth extra, 12s.

Archdeacon Denison.

NOTES OF MY LIFE, 1805—1878. By George Anthony Denison, Vicar of East Brent, 1845: Archdeacon of Taunton, 1851. Third Edition, 8vo., cloth, 12s.

Bishop Herbert de Losinga.

THE FOUNDER OF NORWICH CATHEDRAL. The LIFE, LETTERS, and SERMONS of BISHOP HERBERT DE LOSINGA (b. circ. A.D. 1050, d. 1119). By Edward Meyrick Goulburn, D.D., Dean of Norwich, and Henry Symonds, M.A. 2 vols., 8vo., cloth, 30s.

John Armstrong.

LIFE OF JOHN ARMSTRONG, D.D., late Lord Bishop of Grahamstown. By the Rev. T. T. Carter, M.A., Rector of Clewer. Third Edition. Fcap. 8vo., with Portrait, cloth, 7s. 6d.

Bishop Wilson.

THE LIFE OF THE RIGHT REVEREND FATHER IN GOD, THOMAS WILSON, D.D., Lord Bishop of Sodor and Man. By the late Rev. John Keble, M.A., Vicar of Hursley. 2 vols., 8vo., cloth, £1 1s.

THE SAINTLY LIFE OF MRS. MARGARET GODOLPHIN. 16mo., 1s.

FOOTPRINTS ON THE SANDS OF TIME. Biographies for Young People. Fcap., limp cloth, 2s. 6d.

THE AUTHORIZED EDITIONS OF

THE CHRISTIAN YEAR,

With the Author's latest Corrections and Additions.

NOTICE.—Messrs. PARKER are the sole Publishers of the Editions of the "Christian Year" issued with the sanction and under the direction of the Author's representatives. All Editions without their imprint are unauthorized.

	s. d.		*s. d.*
Handsomely printed on toned paper. SMALL 4to. EDITION.		32mo. EDITION.	
		Cloth, limp	1 0
Cloth extra . . . 10 6		Cloth boards, gilt edges .	1 6
DEMY 8vo. EDITION. Cloth	6 0	48mo. EDITION.	
		Cloth, limp	0 6
FCAP. 8vo. EDITION. Cloth	3 6	Roan	1 6
		FACSIMILE OF THE 1ST EDI-	
24mo. EDIT. With red lines, cl. 2 6		TION. 2 vols., 12mo., boards	7 6

The above Editions are kept in a variety of bindings.

By the same Author.

LYRA INNOCENTIUM. Thoughts in Verse on Christian Children. *Thirteenth Edition.* Fcap. 8vo., cloth, 5s.
———————— 48mo. edition, limp cloth, 6d. ; cloth boards, 1s.
MISCELLANEOUS POEMS by the Rev. JOHN KEBLE, M.A., Vicar of Hursley. *Third Edition.* Fcap. cloth, 6s.
THE PSALTER OR PSALMS OF DAVID : In English Verse. *Fourth Edition.* Fcap., cloth, 6s.

The above may also be had in various bindings.

By the late Rev. ISAAC WILLIAMS.

THE CATHEDRAL ; or, The Catholic and Apostolic Church in England. Fcap. 8vo., cloth, 5s.; 32mo., cloth, 2s. 6d.
THE BAPTISTERY ; or, The Way of Eternal Life. Fcap. 8vo., cloth, 7s. 6d. (with the Plates); 32mo., cloth, 2s. 6d.
HYMNS translated from the PARISIAN BREVIARY. 32mo., cloth, 2s. 6d.
THE CHRISTIAN SCHOLAR. Fcap. 8vo., cloth, 5s. ; 32mo., cloth, 2s. 6d.
THOUGHTS IN PAST YEARS. 32mo., cloth, 2s. 6d.
THE SEVEN DAYS ; or, The Old and New Creation. Fcap. 8vo., cloth, 3s. 6d.

CHRISTIAN BALLADS AND POEMS.

By ARTHUR CLEVELAND COXE, D.D., Bishop of Western New York. A New Edition, printed in Red and Black, Fcap. 8vo., cloth, 2s. 6d.—Cheap Edition, 1s.

The POEMS of GEORGE HERBERT.

THE TEMPLE. Sacred Poems and Private Ejaculations. A New Edition, in Red and Black, 24mo., cloth, 2s. 6d.—Cheap Edition, 1s.

THE ARCHBISHOP OF CANTERBURY.

SINGLEHEART. By Dr. EDWARD WHITE BENSON, Archbishop of Canterbury, late Bishop of Truro, &c. ADVENT SERMONS, 1876, preached in Lincoln Cathedral. Second Edition. Crown 8vo., cloth, 2s. 6d.

THE BISHOP OF SALISBURY.

UNIVERSITY SERMONS ON GOSPEL SUBJECTS. By the Right Rev. the LORD BISHOP OF SALISBURY. Fcap. 8vo., cl., 2s. 6d.

THE LATE BISHOP OF SALISBURY.

SERMONS ON THE BEATITUDES, with others mostly preached before the University of Oxford; to which is added a Preface relating to the volume of "Essays and Reviews." New Edition. Crown 8vo., cloth, 7s. 6d.

THE BISHOP OF NEWCASTLE.

THE AWAKING SOUL. As sketched in the 130th Psalm. Addresses delivered at St. Peter's, Eaton-square, on the Tuesdays in Lent, 1877, by E. R. WILBERFORCE, M.A. [Rt. Rev. the Lord Bp. of Newcastle]. Crown 8vo., limp cloth, 2s. 6d.

THE BISHOP OF BARBADOS.

SERMONS PREACHED ON SPECIAL OCCASIONS. By JOHN MITCHINSON, D.D., late Bishop of Barbados. Crown 8vo., cloth, 5s.

VERY REV. THE DEAN OF CHICHESTER.

SHORT SERMONS FOR FAMILY READING, following the Course of the Christian Seasons. By Very Rev. J. W. BURGON, B.D., Dean of Chichester. First Series. 2 vols., Fcap. 8vo., cloth, 8s.
—— SECOND SERIES. 2 vols., Fcap. 8vo., cloth, 8s.

VERY REV. THE DEAN OF ROCHESTER.

HINTS TO PREACHERS, ILLUSTRATED BY SERMONS AND ADDRESSES. By S. REYNOLDS HOLE, Dean of Rochester. Second Edition. Post 8vo., cloth, 6s.

REV. J. KEBLE.

SERMONS, OCCASIONAL AND PAROCHIAL. By the late Rev. JOHN KEBLE, M.A., Vicar of Hursley. 8vo., cloth, 12s.

THE REV. CANON PAGET.

THE REDEMPTION OF WORK. ADDRESSES spoken in St. Paul's Cathedral, by FRANCIS PAGET, M.A., Senior Student of Christ Church, Oxford. 52 pp. Fcap. 8vo., cloth, 2s.

CONCERNING SPIRITUAL GIFTS. Three Addresses to Candidates for Holy Orders in the Diocese of Ely. With a Sermon. By FRANCIS PAGET, M.A., Senior Student of Christ Church, Oxford. Fcap. 8vo., cloth, 2s. 6d.

Works of the Standard English Divines,

PUBLISHED IN THE LIBRARY OF ANGLO-CATHOLIC THEOLOGY.

Andrewes' (Bp.) Complete Works. 11 vols., 8vo., £3 7s.
THE SERMONS. (Separate.) 5 vols., £1 15s.

Beveridge's (Bp.) Complete Works. 12 vols., 8vo., £4 4s.
THE ENGLISH THEOLOGICAL WORKS. 10 vols., £3 10s.

Bramhall's (Abp.) Works, with Life and Letters, &c.
5 vols., 8vo., £1 15s.

Bull's (Bp.) Harmony on Justification. 2 vols., 8vo., 10s.
——————— **Defence of the Nicene Creed.** 2 vols., 10s.
——————— **Judgment of the Catholic Church.** 5s.

Cosin's (Bp.) Works Complete. 5 vols., 8vo., £1 10s.

Crakanthorp's Defensio Ecclesiæ Anglicanæ. 8vo., 7s.

Frank's Sermons. 2 vols., 8vo., 10s.

Forbes' Considerationes Modestæ. 2 vols., 8vo., 12s.

Gunning's Paschal, or Lent Fast. 8vo., 6s.

Hammond's Practical Catechism. 8vo., 5s.
——————— **Miscellaneous Theological Works.** 5s.
——————— **Thirty-one Sermons.** 2 Parts. 10s.

Hickes's Two Treatises on the Christian Priesthood.
3 vols., 8vo., 15s.

Johnson's (John) Theological Works. 2 vols., 8vo., 10s.
——————— **English Canons.** 2 vols., 12s.

Laud's (Abp.) Complete Works. 7 vols., (9 Parts,) 8vo.,
£2 17s.

L'Estrange's Alliance of Divine Offices. 8vo., 6s.

Marshall's Penitential Discipline. 8vo., 4s.

Nicholson's (Bp.) Exposition of the Catechism. (This
volume cannot be sold separate from the complete set.)

Overall's (Bp.) Convocation-book of 1606. 8vo., 5s.

Pearson's (Bp.) Vindiciæ Epistolarum S. Ignatii.
2 vols., 8vo., 10s.

Thorndike's (Herbert) Theological Works Complete.
· 6 vols., (10 Parts,) 8vo., £2 10s.

Wilson's (Bp.) Works Complete. With **Life,** by Rev.
J. KEBLE. 7 vols., (8 Parts,) 8vo., £3 3s.

** *The 81 Vols. in 88, for £15 15s. net.*

HISTORICAL TALES,

Illustrating the Chief Events in Ecclesiastical History
British and Foreign, &c.

Fcap. 8vo., 1s. each Tale, or 3s. 6d. each Volume in cloth.

ENGLAND. Vol. I.

1.— THE CAVE IN THE HILLS ; or, Cæcilius Viriathus.
5.—WILD SCENES AMONGST THE CELTS.
7.—THE RIVALS : A Tale of the Anglo-Saxon Church.
10.—THE BLACK DANES.
14.—THE ALLELUIA BATTLE ; or, Pelagianism in Britain.

ENGLAND. Vol. II.

16.—ALICE OF FOBBING ; or, The Times of Jack Straw and Wat Tyler.
18.—AUBREY DE L'ORNE ; or, The Times of St. Anselm.
21. — THE FORSAKEN ; or, The Times of St. Dunstan.
24.—WALTER THE ARMOURER ; or, The Interdict.
27.—AGNES MARTIN ; or, The Fall of Cardinal Wolsey.

AMERICA AND OUR COLONIES.

3.—THE CHIEF'S DAUGHTER ; or, The Settlers in Virginia.
8.—THE CONVERT OF MASSACHU-SETTS.
20.—WOLFINGHAM ; or, The Convict Settler of Jervis Bay.
25.—THE CATECHUMENS OF THE COROMANDEL COAST.
28.—ROSE AND MINNIE ; or, The Loyalist : A Tale of Canada in 1837.

FRANCE AND SPAIN.

2.—THE EXILES OF THE CEBENNA ; a Journal written during the Decian Persecution.
22.—THE DOVE OF TABENNA ; and THE RESCUE.
23.—LARACHE : A Tale of the Portuguese Church in the Sixteenth Century.
29.—DORES DE GUALDIM : A Tale of the Portuguese Revolution.

EASTERN AND NORTHERN EUROPE.

6.—THE LAZAR-HOUSE OF LEROS : a Tale of the Eastern Church.
11.—THE CONVERSION OF ST. VLAdimir ; or, The Martyrs of Kief.
13.—THE CROSS IN SWEDEN ; or,The Days of King Ingi the Good.
17.—THE NORTHERN LIGHT : A Tale of Iceland and Greenland.
26.—THE DAUGHTERS OF POLA ; a Tale of the Great Tenth Persecution.

ASIA AND AFRICA.

4.—THE LILY OF TIFLIS : a Sketch from Georgian Church History.
9.—THE QUAY OF THE DIOSCURI : a Tale of Nicene Times.
12.—THE SEA-TIGERS : A Tale of Mediæval Nestorianism.
15.—THE BRIDE OF RAMCUTTAH : A Tale of the Jewish Missions.
19.—LUCIA'S MARRIAGE ; or, The Lions of Wady-Araba.

The late Dr. Elvey's Psalter.

Just published, 16mo.. cloth, 1s. ; by Post, 1s. 2d.
A CHEAP EDITION (being the 20th) of
THE PSALTER ; or, Canticles and Psalms of David.
Pointed for Chanting on a New Principle. With Explanations and Directions. By the late STEPHEN ELVEY, Mus. Doc., Organist of New and St. John's Colleges, and Organist and Choragus to the University of Oxford. With a Memorandum on the Pointing of the *Gloria Patri*, by Sir G. J. ELVEY.

Also,

II. FCAP. 8vo. EDITION (the 21st), limp cloth, 2s. 6d. With PROPER PSALMS. 3s.
III. LARGE TYPE EDITION for ORGAN (the 18th). Demy 8vo., cloth, 5s.
THE PROPER PSALMS separately. Fcap. 8vo. sewed, 6d.
THE CANTICLES separately (18th Edition). Fcap. 8vo., 3d.
The Psalter is used at St. George's Chapel, Windsor, and at many Cathedrals.

OXFORD AND LONDON : PARKER AND CO.